AWS

The Ultimate Cheat Sheet Practice Exam
Questions

(Prepare for and Pass the Current Aws Machine
Learning Specialty Exam)

Victor Bradley

Published By **Victor Bradley**

Victor Bradley

*Aws: The Ultimate Cheat Sheet Practice Exam Questions
(Prepare for and Pass the Current Aws Machine Learning
Specialty Exam)*

ISBN 978-1-77485-427-3

Legal & Disclaimer

The information contained in this book is not designed to replace or take the place of any form of medicine or professional medical advice. The information in this book has been provided for educational and entertainment purposes only.

The information contained in this book has been compiled from sources deemed reliable, and it is accurate to the best of the Author's knowledge; however, the Author cannot guarantee its accuracy and validity and cannot be held liable for any errors or omissions. Changes are periodically made to this book. You must consult your doctor or get professional medical advice before using any of the suggested remedies, techniques, or information in this book.

Upon using the information contained in this book, you agree to hold harmless the Author from and against any damages, costs, and expenses, including any legal fees potentially resulting from the application of any of the information provided by this guide. This disclaimer applies to any damages or injury caused by the use and application, whether directly or indirectly, of any advice or information presented, whether for breach of contract, tort, negligence, personal injury, criminal intent, or under any other cause of action.

You agree to accept all risks of using the information presented inside this book. You need to consult a professional medical practitioner in order to ensure you are both able and healthy enough to participate in this program.

TABLE OF CONTENTS

Introduction

AWS provides many web-based services. We'll discuss these within this guide. Cloud computing in simple terms, refers to storage and processing of data and services on the Internet and not on the hard drive in your personal computer.

Your hard drive is what cloud computing isn't all about. This is known as local computing and storage, when you store data or run programs on the hard drive. Everything you require is located close to your that means you'll can access quickly and easily to your information (for the one device or for those connected to networks that are local to you). Working off of your hard disk is the way that the technology industry has operated for the last decade.

Computing technology's future is on the cloud. That means that if not adjusting your business to the cloud-based model, your company is going to be out in this age of technology advancement.

Cloud computing refers to the process of having organizations connect to a network of accessible servers. Servers are stored on Internet which allows organizations to manage their information "in the cloud" instead of local servers. It's a virtual area where devices on the network can access information from any location.

Cloud computing has just seen a significant increase in popularity over the past two years in the last decade or two, the idea has been in existence for a long time. John McCarthy, a renowned computer scientist, first introduced the concept in the form of the technology that allowed computation to be advertised as a product, such as water or electricity. He stated that subscribers would only pay for the amount they actually used , and that some users could offer services to others.

Amazon Web Services can be described as a powerful cloud platform designed by Amazon's online retailer. It provides software-as-as-a-Service (SaaS) Platform-as as-a-Service (PaaS) and infrastructure-as-as-a-Service (IaaS) solutions. Consider the past of electricity to comprehend the logic behind AWS.

At first, factories would construct their own facilities to power their factories. In the course of time, both private and public investors have built large power stations that provide electricity to many cities, factories, and homes. In this new arrangement factories will pay much less per unit due in the economics of scale that are facilitated by these massive power plants. AWS was created and constructed using similar principles.

In the year 2006, Amazon had established itself as the world's biggest internet retailer. A title it continues to hold. Running a massive operation requires a huge and advanced infrastructure. Amazon was infused Amazon with deep understanding of managing large-scale network and servers.

In the end, AWS was created in 2006 when Amazon endeavored to make available to both individuals and businesses the technology infrastructure it built and the experience it acquired. AWS was among the first pay-as you-go (PAYG) computer models to increase the performance as well as storage and computing in accordance with the changing requirements that the customer.

Amazon Web Services offers cloud infrastructure that includes numerous data centers as well as various accessibility zones (AZs) covering regions across the globe. Each AZ comprises a range of centers. Customers are able to set up virtual machines and store their data across multiple AZs to create an extremely scalable network that is invulnerable to problems with data centers.

Chapter 1: The Essentials

Welcome to the very beginning section of this book. This chapter covers the essential basics needed to begin by introducing the essentials you need to know in order to use Amazon Web Services.

Client-Server Technology

Client-Server technology is a technique to isolate the capabilities in an application to two specific components. Client-server represents the relationship between two PC applications where one program is called the client. The client sends requests for services from another program, called the server, and it fulfills the demand. The client displays and manages the information on the computer. The server functions as a central computer to save and retrieve protected information. It's a network-based system where every operation within the network is either a client or server. Servers are amazing computers or processes dedicated to managing printers, disk drives (print servers) as well as network servers.

In addition, Clients are workstations that users have the authority to run programs. Clients depend on servers to store reasons like devices and files.

Clients and servers typically share the same information through PCs that connect to unconnected hardware, however, both be based on the same framework. The host machine is server running at least one server program that share their characteristics with clients.

A client isn't sharing its property, yet it needs information from servers. Clients, as a result begin correspondence with servers waiting for any requests that come in.

The nature of the client-server illustrates the relationship between the applications in. Servers provide ability or service a few or many customers who begin with their needs for services.

Capabilities for example, trading email, Internet access, and databases, are compiled based on the model of client-server. For instance, a web-based program is a program that runs on a PC of a user that is able to access data from a web server, or via the Internet. This program can, in turn send the information to the program database client, which transmits the request to a database of a server located on another computer to retrieve ledger information.

The model of the client-server has become one of the main ideas of the field of network computing. A variety of business applications nowadays use the model of the client-server. In the marketing the concept, it has been applied to distinguish disseminated computing on pocket-sized PCs as distinct from "computing" robust , integrated central PCs.

Every instance of programming for clients can make request for information to at minimum one server. In this way, servers will be able to acknowledge the requests, process them and then return the requested information back to the user. While this notion is applicable to a variety of reasons behind different kinds of use cases, the design remains in the general sense of the concept of equivalence.

The client-server model comes with the three distinct segments, each of which focuses on a particular activity:

* Database server

* Client application

* Network

Database Server

A server handles properties, such as the databases, which are effectively and in ideally, across multiple clients who also require the server to handle similar properties. The database server focuses on the obligations that go with it.

* Management of an individual database of information across multiple concurrent clients.

Controlling the entry of databases and other security needs.

* Protecting databases from information with backup and recovery highlights.

Centrally maintaining the global information quality can lead to client-facing applications.

Client Application

Client applications are an element of the framework clients use to communicate with data. The client application within the model of a server-client client spotlights the activities that go with it:

* Displaying some interfaces between clients and property to complete the job.

* Managing the report's the rationale behind it, applying the reasoning, and Validating information section.

* Controlling the request traffic for accepting and transmitting data from the database server

Network

The third component of a client-server framework the network. Correspondence programming acts as the mechanism that transmits data between clients and servers within the framework of a client-server. Both the client and server are running correspondence software which allows them to communicate through the network.

The Merits and the Demerits in Client-Server Model

The main advantage of the model of client-server because of its unifying design, which makes it simpler to secure that access controls for information are complied with by security methods. It doesn't matter any difference if the client and servers are based on the same framework because information is passed through protocols for client-server that are stage-skeptical.

One of the major drawbacks of the model client-server is that when many clients require information from the server at once it could be a burden. This could lead to a situation referred to as "network clog" the sheer volume of requests can result in an end of service.

Protocols for client-server

Clients typically talk to servers through the protocols suite of TCP/IP. TCP is an association-configured protocol. This means that an association is established and maintained until applications at both ends are finished with trading messages. It determines the method of breaking applications into packets that network can transmit, and is responsible for sending packets for acknowledging and transferring packets sent from the network layer. In addition, it also manages stream control and manages the retransmission of damaged packets to confirm every packet which show up. Within the Open Network Interconnection correspondence model, TCP covers portions of Layer 4, the Transport Layer as well as a part of Layer 5 which is which is the Session Layer.

In contrast, IP is a connectionless protocol, meaning that there is no way to establish the connection between the ends that are communicating. Every packet sent through the Internet is considered to be an unattached unit of data that is not connected to any other data group.

The Difference Between the Client Server Computing and Peer to Peer Computing

The main differences between peer-to-peer computing are according to the following:

In the world of client-server computing, the server functions as a central hub that provides services to numerous client hubs. In peer-to-peer computing system hub, all hubs use their capabilities and interact with each other.

*Client-Server computing has been accepted as a subcategory of peer-to-peer computing.

*In the world of client-server computing the server is the one who communicates with various hubs. In peer-to-peer

computing, all hubs are identical and share information to one another in a simple manner.

Servers with different types

I. File Server

*File Servers are useful for sharing data on the network

* The client transmits the request to record a document through an interface to an account in the server.

File servers are considered as the simplest kind of information system used to trade messages on the internet to find the data mentioned.

The file servers grant access to distant server's processors. When running software, shared data such as databases, backups and databases are stored on disks as well as optical storage devices that are managed by the server for file.

II. Database Server

*The client sends the SQL requests in the form of messages sent to the server for database. the outcome of every SQL request is sent to the network.

*The code that is the SQL request and the data is located in the same machine and the server uses its preparing capabilities to discover the requested information and return it to the client instead of transferring all accounts back to the user. This leads to a greater efficiency in the use of circulation of handling power.

*Take note this: the code for your application is on the client. Along these lines, you must consider writing code to the client. Alternatively, you could purchase an inquiry tool that is shrink wrapped.

The databases servers offer the opportunity to select support networks, and perform an essential job in information warehousing.

III. Transaction Servers

The client can access remote methods or services which reside on the server by using an SQL database motor that is connected to an exchange server.

Network trade is comprised of one request and response. The SQL proclamations can either be successful or failed as a whole.

*When you use the Transaction Server, it is possible to create the client-server application by writing codes for the server as well as the server segments.

The client component includes the Graphical User Interface (GUI) and the server component includes SQL exchanges with databases. These are known as Online Transaction Processing.

These are applications that require a shorter reaction time, typically around 1-to-3 seconds.

*OLTP applications also require ongoing control in the area of security and trustworthiness that the databases have.

IV. Groupware Servers

It consists of the administration of semi-organized information, for instance, images, content notice sheets, mail and the flow of work.

*This framework puts people directly in contact with other users. The most effective models comprise Lotus Notes and Microsoft Exchange.

*Groupware-specific programming may be built on a seller's pre-configured configuration of client-server APIs. A majority of the time, apps are created using an underlying scripting language as well as structured interfaces offered to the vendor. Nowadays, many groupware products make use of email as an information-sharing middleware. In addition the Internet is fast becoming the primary middleware base for groupware.

V. O.A. Servers.

*The client-server program comprises a great deal of discussing objects using the help of an object server.

*Client object makes use of an Object Request Broker (ORB) for the purpose of being able to communicate with server objects.

*The ORB detects an instance of the class object server it then invokes the method described and reports the results for the object of client.

*Server objects should assist in sharing and simultaneous angles. The ORB and a different age of CORBA application servers unite all of the above.

*The ORB's for businesses which accept the OMG's CORBA standard includes the following , including Iona's DAIS and Java Soft's Java IDL, and Expersoft's Powerbroker.

VI. Web Application Server

Web application servers are a different kind that is part of Internet programming. They combine the traditional HTTP servers by incorporating segments that are server-side. In essence, they are similar to object servers.

*This type of client-server is comprised of small, flexible in addition to "widespread" clients who engage in conversation with super-fast servers. This is where the Web server provides archives whenever clients ask for them using their names. Both the clients and the servers transmit data using a protocol similar to protocol known as HTTP that is simple set of directions, parameters that are transmitted in strings, without agreement on the composition of data.

*In the case of Microsoft it was the Multi-Tasking Staff disseminated the object server. But due to CORBA/Java Enterprise JavaBeans has been the most common exchange for Web Application servers.

*A few of these servers also offer the CORBA/COM/COM spans.

ORB

It can be described as an object request broker (ORB) that is a middleware technology which manages the exchange of information and correspondence between objects. ORB is the name of the object transport. It lets objects easily send a request to and then receive responses from the various items that are located either locally or remotely. The client isn't aware of the mechanisms used to communicate with and initiate or store server objects. CORBA ORB CORBA ORB gives a vibrant configuration of dispersed middleware. A ORB is significantly more advanced than the other forms of middleware for client-servers, such as protocols like Remote Procedure Calls (RPC's) as well as Message-Oriented Midware (MOM) and database-stored method, and cloud services. CORBA is the most efficient middleware that a client can use at any time defined.

ORBs enhance the interoperability of disseminated object structures since they allow clients to build frameworks by separating objects from various vendors that can communicate with each other using the ORB.

ORB technology is advancing the goal of object correspondence between the programming, machine, and even the merchant's limits.

The components in an ORB technology include:

* Interface definition

*Location and possible activation of remote devices

* Communication among clients . the item

Obligations of the ORB

*Giving the illusion of locality The ORB is required to create an illusion of location, so in order to make it appear in a way that it appears as if the object is located in the user, even though in reality it may be in a different process or machine.

*Disable the details of implementation The next, more advanced step towards interoperations between objects that is the exchange of an object across different phases. An ORB lets an object conceal the details of its execution from users. It can include programming languages, working frameworks, and even the size of the object. Every one of these can be regarded as a "straightforwardness," and diverse ORB advances may decide to help various transparencies, accordingly broadening the advantages of object direction across stages and correspondence channels.

There are a variety of ways to realizing the fundamental ORB concept. For example, ORB capacities can be combined into clients, could be separate processes, or be part of a working framework. These basic structure options could be incorporated into a single item, or it could be a variety of options made by those who are the ORB implementer.

There are Two Significant ORB Technologies:

*Object Management Group's (OMG) Common Object Request Broker Style (CORBA).

Microsoft's Component Object Model (COM).

Communication Network

In the world of PCs Networking is the process of connecting two or more computers to share data. Networks can be accessed using the combination of PC hardware as well as PC-based programming. Networks can be classified in various ways. One approach is to define the kind of network based on the geographical area that it covers. However networks can also be classified based on topology or kinds of protocols that they support.

Introduction to Network Type

One way to categorize the various kinds of PC networks is through their size or extension. In fact the industry of networking refers to virtually every kind of structure, including one of the area networks.

Network Types Include:

*Local Area Network * - Local Area Network

*WLAN Wireless Local Area Network LAN - - Wide Area Network

* MAN - Metropolitan Area Network

*SAN *SAN Storage Area Network Network Area Network, Server Area

Network, or in certain instances Small Area Network

*PAN Personal Area Network Personal Area Network

*DAN Desk Area Network Desk Area Network

Local Area Network is a contraction of Local Area Network

A LAN connects a network device with a generally brief distance. A place of business that is networked or school or at home typically has an individual LAN, but every now and then, a structure might include a couple of smaller LANs. And occasionally, a LAN may traverse an array of nearby structures. In TCP/IP networking, a network is usually, but not run continuously as one IP subnet. The LAN is often associated with other LANs and connects to the Internet or another internet-connected WANs. Local network operators use mostly small-sized equipment, such as Ethernet connections as well as network connectors and centers. Remote LAN and various other advanced LAN equipment options also are available. The most popular type that is a local area network known as an Ethernet LAN. The smallest home network can contain just two PCs and a large LAN may require a huge number of computers.

Metropolitan Area Network

MAN can be described as a system that spans an area of physical size than a LAN, but less than a WAN, as an instance an urban area. It is a Metropolitan Area Network is ordinarily owned and operated by one person such as the administrative body or a major organization.

Wide Area Network - Wide Area Network

WAN is a huge physical divide. It is the Internet is the largest WAN that spans the entire globe.

Different types of Network Protocols.

In the world in technology there exist huge numbers of users who communicate with different devices in diverse languages. It also remembers a variety of methods of transmitting information in conjunction with the different programs they implement. In this way, sharing information globally wouldn't be possible without standardised 'norms' to control how the client communicates information, just like how our devices handle this information.

I'll be focusing more about "protocols," which are an instruction set which help to manage the manner in which a particular technology can be used to communicate. It is generally believed that these protocols are modern dialects that are augmented by networking calculations. There are many networks and protocols which users can use when surfing.

There are various kinds of protocols that perform in a huge and exemplary job in communicating with various devices over the internet. They include:

* Transmission Control Protocol (TCP)

* Internet Protocol (IP)

* The User Datagram Protocol (UDP)

* Post Office Protocol (POP)

* Simple mail transport Protocol (SMTP)

* * Transfer Protocol (FTP)

* Hypertext Transfer Protocol (HTTP)

* Hypertext Transfer Protocol Secure (HTTPS)

*

Here, I'll briefly talk about each:

* Transmission Control Protocol (TCP): TCP is a well-known protocol for correspondence that is used to transmit information over networks. It breaks down any message into a sequence of packets sent from source to destination and is then rebuilt at the point of delivery.

*Internet Protocol (IP): IP is clearly structured in the way it addresses the protocol and in the majority of cases it is used in conjunction with TCP. The IP addresses contained in packets aid in routing them through different hubs within the network until it lands at the network of choice. TCP/IP is the most widely-known protocol for connecting to networks.

*User Datagram Protocol (UDP): UDP is a substitute correspondence protocol for Transmission Control Protocol that was developed to create loss-bearing and low-inactivity between different applications.

*Post Office Protocol (POP) POP3 is designed to accept emails from incoming E-mails.

* Simple Mail Transport Protocol (SMTP): SMTP is designed to distribute and send active E-Mail.

*File Transfer Protocol (FTP) FTP allows clients to transfer documents from one computer and moving to the next. Account types can include program accounts as well as content documents, archives, and so on.

*Hypertext Transfer Protocol (HTTP): HTTP is intended to move hypertext across at least two networks. HTML labels are utilized for joining. These connections can be made any kind of structure, such as images or text. HTTP is built on Client-server standards that allow clients to set up an affiliation with the server to make requests. The server is aware of the request made by the user and responds in a manner that is appropriate.

*Hypertext Transfer Protocol Secure (HTTPS): HTTPS is truncated to Hypertext Transfer Protocol Secure, and is a common protocol to ensure that communications are established between two computers using the program and the second receiving details from the Webserver. HTTP is used to move information between the client program (demand) as well as the server (reaction) using the hypertext format, apart from the movement of data that is performed in an encrypted position. Therefore, it can be said that https prevent hackers in their understanding of or manipulation of information by transferring packets.

Chapter 2: What Exactly Is Cloud Computing?

The majority of IT solutions are branded with the word "cloud computing" or cloud solution. These buzzwords can be helpful to sales, but they can be difficult to incorporate into the form of a book. To make things clearer we'll define some terms.

The cloud computing metaphor is to describe the consumption and provision of computing resources. Cloud computing resources aren't immediately visible to users there exist layers of abstraction in between the two. The degree of abstraction provided by cloud computing differs, in the form of virtual computers (VMs) to offering software as service (SaaS) that is based on complex distributed systems. The cloud's resources are available in large quantities , and you pay only for the resources you need.

Cloud computing refers to two software applications that are available as Internet services as well as the software and hardware systems of data centers that offer these services. The data center's hardware and software is what we refer to as cloud. Cloud computing is new concept that is now becoming well-known. Cloud computing takes advantage of technology that allows virtualization. at the core the concept of cloud computing there's an apparent separation of the various nodes. Each node appears to be a distinct physical machine that the user can use. In contrast to grid computing, many distributed computers are linked with one another, creating one large logical system capable of handling large quantities of computations and data. For cloud computing virtualization technology makes every node appear to be a distinct physical machine. This allows users to install custom operating systems and software at every node and create specific rules for each node.

The concept of cloud computing is derived out of parallel transforms or ordered distribution, and grid computing. There are some similarities between the three, however they function in different ways. While cloud computing is a relatively new field that is competing, this concept has been in use for a long time. Cloud computing is because applications and data are in the "cloud" made up of Web servers. To simplify the idea cloud competition, it can be described as sharing applications and resources within an environment of network to work without having to worry about ownership and control of the networks resources and applications. According to Scale, when you use cloud computing it means that the IT resources required to accomplish the task and your information are no longer saved on a personal computer instead, they are stored in a different location to be accessible any time, anywhere.

and launch a geophysical modeling application, which is accessible everywhere. This may include the capability to lease the virtual server, turn the software on, turn off or disable it at any time or even clone it to handle a sudden increase in workload. This could include warehousing and protecting large quantities of data that are only accessible to users who are authorized and apps. It could be compatible with a cloud provider who sets up a platform to automatically adapt to any changes to the work. This could involve the use of a cloud storage service to store business, applications as well as personal information. This could include the possibility of using many web services to integrate images, maps and GPS information in order to build pages for customers' browsers.

In cloud computing systems the load is dramatically changed. Local computers do not require to run software. Cloud computing networks handle instead. In this scenario the need for hardware and software by the user is decreased. Let the cloud manage. The sole thing local computers need to be aware of is the interface software that runs the application. Today, web browsers such as Mozilla Firefox or Internet Explorer 8 is widely employed as an interface software for cloud compatibility systems. It is a fact that Internet users have used various forms of cloud computing. If you've got an email account using an online email service like Hotmail, Yahoo! Mail, or Gmail I have experienced some cloud computing. In lieu of running an email application on a local machine it connects remotely to an online account. Account storage and software is not available locally on the computer but is instead in cloud services.

Three distinct aspects differentiate cloud computing as opposed to conventional hosting. It is first, it is offered at a cost per minute or per hour. It is also flexible. Users can avail all or a portion of services at any point. The cloud computing service is entirely managed by the service provider. Recent advances in the field of distributed computing and virtualization and improved accessibility to the Internet has led to a rise in interest in cloud computing.

Cloud computing has revolutionized how we design and deploy software. Through Amazon Web Services's cloud-based marketing service, users are able to trade customized hardware and infrastructure virtual servers, and quickly manage storage, security, and networking services. You only pay per CPU you require. Learn some tricks and strategies and you'll be certain that your apps will be running on AWS within minutes.

Clouds that are private, public, or hybrid cloud

In essence, there are three kinds of cloud cloud computing: private, public as well as hybrid clouds. In a cloud that is public, external service providers provide the resources and services accessible to their customers via the Internet. Applications and data of customers are stored on an infrastructure that is that is owned and controlled of the company providing the services. Private cloud provides numerous of the advantages as a cloud that is public however the data and services are managed by the business or a third-party only for the use of the customer. It is generally true that private clouds on cloud services will increase the cost of administration for the client, yet allow more control over the infrastructure, and decrease security issues. The infrastructure is able to be placed within or outside of the company's structures.

The hybrid cloud can be described as a mix between a cloud that is private as well as an open cloud. The choice on what functions between the cloud that is private as well as the cloud that is public generally dependent on several aspects, such as the commercial significance that the app has, as well as the security of the data, necessary certifications and standards for industry and regulations, etc. In some instances the peak periods of demand for resources can be controlled by the cloud public.

Cloud computing is usually described by the three different types of services, including IaaS, PaaS and SaaS in which aaS is an abbreviation for "as as a service" and the term "service" means that the service isn't restricted to the user's location but the location. in a remote location accessible via a network). The letters I, P , and S in acronyms are used to refer to different kinds of functionality as the following table clearly illustrates:

Infrastructure as a Service (Iaas) It provides users with the fundamental concepts of computing, including Transformation, connectivity to networks, and storage. (Of course, you'll require additional features to support IaaS functions like account management, user tracking and even security). You must use an IaaS cloud service provider if you intend to build your own application and require access to the low-level functions of your operating system.

Platform as a Service (PaaS) instead of providing basic features within an operating system, PaaS gives high-level programming frameworks that developers interact to access IT services. For instance, instead opening a file, and writing bits into it in the PaaS setting, the programmer simply calls a function , and then delivers the bits collection. The PaaS structure is able to handle the work of like creating the document, writing bits, and verifying that it has been received by the system. It is the PaaS infrastructure service provider accountable for keeping backups of data and storing backups, for instance, to keep the user from having to perform other tasks that require a lot of effort.

Software as a Service (SaaS) is a term that has been developed to a new level with the development of PaaS. With SaaS it is possible to have all the features of the software are delivered via a network in a single package. The user is required to sign up for the service; The SaaS provider takes care of concerns related to the development and running of the application, the segregation of user information and the security of every user, and the overall SaaS environment and the handling of numerous other. details.

As with all models this division of I P and S is a way to explain influence , and aims to create the cleanliness and cleanliness an aspect which, in reality can be quite difficult to understand. For IPS this model appears as though the kinds were correctly defined, even though. Cloud providers typically offer a range of kinds of services. Amazon particularly has been able to offer various platforms-based services as it expands its offerings and also expand into full-featured applications that are offered in conjunction with SaaS. It can be said that Amazon offers all three kinds of cloud computing.

Cloud computing vs cloud computing

If you think that the mix of I P and S in the earlier paragraph is unclear, anticipate to be informed about the difference between private and public cloud. Think about what happens next

1. Amazon is the most popular cloud computing company, provides cloud computing that anyone is able to use it.

2. As we considered the new development in Amazon Web Services, many IT firms have been asked about why they couldn't not develop and provide the same service as AWS for their customers located at their respective data centers. This is also known by the name private cloud computing.

3. In line with the current trend, many hosting companies believe that they could offer their customers in IT a separate area in their servers, and permit customers to build clouds there. The concept could also be described as private cloud computing since it is a service that is specifically designed for a particular user. In contrast the data that comes in this private cloud are stored on a shared network, is it actually private?

4. After discovering that businesses could only select either the private or public sector The term "hybrid" was coined to denote firms that utilize both private and public cloud environments.

When you are moving through the cloud, you'll likely see lots of debate about which cloud environment is the most effective. My personal view is that no matter if you're in the public / private hybrid situation public cloud computing will surely become an essential element of every enterprise's IT infrastructure. Furthermore, Amazon will undoubtedly be the most popular provider of public cloud communications. It is sensible to prepare for a future that incorporates AWS.

Cloud computing is the most important function of cloud computing.

There isn't a specific definition or description for cloud-cloud combination. The process of defining the main aspects of Cloud Computing that are based on field practice can take a while. Based on the practices of the design of services and solutions design fields Two key triggers can play an important role in this new phase in cloud computing

Virtual technology

Virtualization technology can be used to control the way an operating system's, middleware and image of the software are processed and transferred to an actual physical machine or a an element of the server stack. Virtualization technology also allows users to reuse licenses for middleware, operating systems or software programs in the event that a subscriber removes their service via the cloud communication platform.

Service Oriented Architecture (SOA).

An architecture that is service-oriented is an array of services. The services are able to communicate. It could be a basic transfer of data, or two or more services that coordinate the process. There are ways to connect the services are needed. The development of a architecture or programming system is now looking at services, in contrast to previous decades many applications that are completely standalone and distinct.

Recently, due to the huge expansion of internet users has led to the massive growth of Internet users and widespread availability of Internet technology means that the usage of software has been reduced. Large companies like Google, Microsoft, Sun and even Amazon are able to provide software-related services rather than selling the software directly to the end user. SOA is a type of software and system design that addresses components reuse, scalability, and the ability to adapt. All of these are essential to companies that want to reduce costs on options instead of purchasing.

The Reasons People Choose Cloud Computing over Dedicated Server:

Its Benefits

Every person has their personal preference, be it how they use technology of figuring or how they can expand the capabilities of Internet technology. The way that people view the benefits of technology depends on the kind of needs they have, and how technology can help them in meeting their needs. In the present, based on the way that each person perceives the convenience of using the technology, its benefit is an aspect.

Many people who use cloud computing and the Internet and its features consider cloud processing to be the method that has many advantages in comparison to its well-known "rival that is the dedicated server. Below are a few of the characteristics which make cloud-based registration more popular than the other.

a. Cloud processing is extremely versatile. Cloud processing is a great option for cloud computing. What you will need is a computer connected to an Internet and you are able to efficiently generate results. It's not like an uncommitted server it is essential to keep your framework with you as all of the data you require are stored on servers.

b. Cloud registering isn't restricted to one resource. Cloud figuring means that you're not limited to using what your dedicated server is able to offer you. With the vast internet's resources Internet it is possible to make many options about where to use your resource.

C. Cloud processing provides greater security than dedicated servers. The Internet is by itself an extremely reliable and solid security. Even though security is not a priority, the problem of being undefended exists the security aspect has been observed for all possible attacks.

Are you currently acquiring funds for data center management or virtual computing? If you're familiar with getting estimates from web-based services offered by the service you use, these steps listed here will help to request quotations to manage services. First of all, the majority of cloud cloud centers as well as services show prices for packages on their websites. You can view the cost or charges for data storage, transfer, and data requests.

It is common to receive a monthly fixed rate to use these types of services. There are also web services and even data centres which charge per usage. It's up to you to choose which services best suits your requirements. If you're an avid user and intend to utilize lots of storage and bandwidth, it's recommended to call the customer service directly. You could obtain a good contract from these firms. There are also web service and data centers providers that have online citation capabilities. Utilize this feature to request a budget for the transfer of data. This service is typically provided for free, so you can get the best price without any worries.

After you've received your budget you may also reach out to the sales department of your provider to determine if you could obtain a lower price. Finding a quote on the management of your data center is simple today. Because of the fierce competition, certain companies let you bargain a lower cost for the services.

Chapter 3: Amazon Web Services (Aws)

AWS (Amazon Web Services) is an extensive growing cloud. This computing system is offered by Amazon which comes with an array of infrastructure to support (IaaS) and the platform to support (PaaS) and packed applications as service (SaaS) options. AWS services offer a variety of organizational tools like services for delivery of content databases, storage for databases, and power.

Amazon Web Services Amazon Web Services are comprised of over 100 services portfolio including infrastructure, databases, compute, management, program development and security. These solutions, according to category comprise:

* Calculate

* Storage databases

* Data direction

* Migration

* Hybrid cloud

* Networking

* Tools for development

* Direction

* Tracking

* Safety

* Governance

* Big data direction

* Analytics

* Artificial Intelligence (AI)

* Mobile growth

* Telling and messages

* Available

Services are offered through Amazon Web Services from heaps of Information Centers spread across accessibility zones (AZs) across the globe. An AZ is a location which includes physical data centers, even when a location comprises a range of AZs within close proximity. A few or a number of access zones are selected by a company for its end clients due to a variety of factors like closeness and conformity. For instance the AWS client can create virtual machines (VMs) and copy data to different AZs in order to build a solid infrastructure that's immune to server failures or even a complete data center. Amazon Elastic Compute Cloud (EC2) is a service that gives virtual servers, also known as cases for the ability to calculate. The EC2 service provides dozens of case types with dimensions and varying abilities, tailored to software and workload types, for example, tasks that are accelerated-computing and memory-intensive. AWS provides an auto Scaling instrument that allows you to scale to ensure that functionality is kept dynamically, and also to improve the overall wellbeing of the instance.

Storage

Amazon Simple Storage Service (S3) allows for scalable item storage for backup of data archives and analytics. IT professionals can store their documents and other data in objects -- which can be as large as 5 GB within S3 buckets. Companies can save money by using S3's Infrequent Access storage option or by using Amazon Glacier for long term cold storage.

Storage is offered via Amazon Elastic Block Store Volumes for permanent data storage that can be utilized with Amazon EC2 cases. Amazon Elastic File System provides controlled cloud-based storage.

The company is able to migrate data using Transfer equipment, such as, Snowmobile and AWS Snowball or use AWS Storage Gateway to empower programs on premises.

Databases, Information Management

AWS's Relational Database Service The Amazon Relational Database Service offers a variety of databases: Oracle, SQL Server, PostgreSQL, MySQL, MariaDB and a prominent private database called Amazon Aurora -- supplies an application for managing relational databases that is available to AWS users. AWS offers NoSQL databases that can be maintained.

An AWS client can use DynamoDB along with Amazon ElastiCache Accelerator as real-time and in-memory caches of information for software. Amazon Redshift supplies a data warehouse that makes it much easier the data analyst to perform tasks in business intelligence.

Migration and hybrid

AWS provides tools and services that are designed to assist Users transfer databases applications, servers and other data to AWS's cloud, which is public. Its Migration Hub offers a location to for managing and tracking the progress of migrations to and from. EC2 Systems Manager assists an IT team in setting up AWS instances, as well as servers.

Amazon has agreements with vendors of technology that various deployments that facilitate. VMware Cloud on AWS brings the core technology of VMware to the AWS cloud and connects it to data. Red Hat Enterprise Linux for Amazon EC2 is the product of a different venture, which extends Red Hat's Operating System to AWS cloud. AWS cloud.

Media

The Amazon Virtual Private Cloud (Amazon VPC) offers an administrator control of the digital network, which makes it possible to use an isolated section of the AWS cloud. AWS provides new tools to security within the VPC.

Traffic is able to balance itself with of the Load Balancing (ELB) program that includes both the program Load Balancer as well as the Network Load Balancer. AWS offers a domain-specific program called Amazon Route 53 that paths users who are not users.

A connect can be made through an IT specialist via A data center to the AWS cloud via AWS Direct Connect.

Developer tools

Programmers can benefit from AWS command-line tools as well as Software Development Kits (SDKs) to build and manage solutions and software. AWS

Command Line Interface AWS Command Line Interface is an Amazon code port. A programmer can also utilize AWS Tools for Powershell to manage clouds from Windows surroundings , and AWS Serverless Program Model to simulate an AWS-like environment to test Lambda functions. AWS SDKs are available for numerous programming languages, including Java, PHP, Python, Node.js, Ruby, C++, Android and iOS.

Amazon API Gateway empowers a development team to create Track, Manage, and manage custom APIs that permit applications or functionality to connect with services. API Gateway manages hundreds of thousands of API calls that are running concurrently in a single.

AWS also offers a comprehensive service for media transcoding, called Amazon Elastic Transcoder. There's it also provides a service to visualize workflows in order to obtain microservices-based software, AWS Measure Functions.

A development team can make a permanent integration and continuous delivery pipelines with service suppliers like:

* AWS CodePipeline

* AWS CodeBuild

* AWS CodeDeploy

* AWS CodeStar

A programmer is able to save code from Git CodeCommit repositories, and also evaluate the performance of any microservices-based applications using AWS X-Ray.

Control and tracking

An administrator can manage and monitor the configuration of cloud sources via AWS Config Rules and AWS Config. These tools, along in conjunction with AWS Trusted Advisor, will aid an IT team avoid faulty configuration and costly cloud sources deployments.

AWS provides a variety of automation tools within its portfolio. Administrators can automate provisioning of infrastructure through AWS CloudFormation templates and utilize AWS OpsWorks along with Chef to automatize the configuration of infrastructure and systems.

An AWS client is able to monitor the health of resources and applications using Amazon CloudWatch in conjunction with AWS Personal Health Dashboard. AWS Personal Health Dashboard, in addition, it can use AWS CloudTrail to track users' actions and the application API (API) requires the auditing.

Governance and safety

AWS offers a range of cloud safety solutions such as access Control as well as AWS Identity which allows administrators to define and control the access of users. Administrators can also set up a user directory with Amazon Cloud Directory, or join cloud tools with the established Microsoft Active Directory using the AWS Directory Service. AWS Organizations allow a business to control and establish guidelines to manage AWS accounts.

The cloud provider has launched tools to automatically evaluate security threats. Amazon Inspector assesses an AWS regarding vulnerabilities that could impact security and compliance. Amazon Macie utilizes machine learning technology to secure cloud information.

AWS provides solutions and programs that offer applications - and hardware-based encryption that protects from DDoS attacks, offer Secure Sockets Layer and Transport Layer Security certificates, and stop potentially harmful traffic from websites. AWS certified users must be able to prove and verify the cloud's technical expertise and methods within AWS environments.

The AWS Management Console is a user-friendly interface for AWS. The control console is used to manage resources within cloud storage , cloud computing as well as safety credentials. AWS console is able to connect with AWS resources.

Data analytics with a significant impact and management

AWS offers a variety of data analytics and program services. Amazon Elastic MapReduce provides a Hadoop frame that can process large amounts of data, while Amazon Kinesis offers several tools to analyze and process streams of data.

AWS Glue can be used to load tasks, while it is the Amazon Elasticsearch Service empowers a log analysis group and jobs using the Elasticsearch software that's open source.

Analysts can use Amazon Athena to get S3 and query information. visualize information.

Artificial intelligence

AWS provides a range in delivery options and AI Version Development Platforms along with a host of apps which are AI-focused. Amazon AI is an Amazon AI package of tools includes Amazon Lex for text and chatbot engineering using voice, Amazon Polly for Indices translation as well as Amazon Rekognition for assessment of facial and visual images. AWS provides the technology needed to build applications that are dependent on machines.

Utilizing AWS Deep Learning AI AMIs (Amazon Machine Pictures) Programmers learn and develop customized AI versions that use GPU clusters, or instances that are optimized for computing. AWS has learning growth frameworks, such as TensorFlow as well as MXNet.

On the other hand AWS technology powers Alexa Voice A, the Alexa Voice A programmer, and services also can use programs created by Alexa Skills Kit. Alexa Skills Kit.

Mobile growth

AWS Mobile Hub AWS Mobile Hub is various solutions and apps, including The AWS Mobile SDK for app developers. It provides code samples and libraries.

A programmer can use Amazon Cognito to manage user access to mobile applications and also Amazon Pinpoint which allows you to issue push notifications to the end-users of programs and assess the effectiveness of these messages.

Alarms and messages

AWS messaging services provide central communications between software and customers. Amazon Simple Queue Service (SQS) is a managed message queue which sends messages to shops as well as receiving messages between components of distributed software, making certain that all the parts of the application function in a planned manner.

Amazon Simple Notification Service (SNS) allows a company to communicate with endpoints, such as solutions or end-users. SNS comprises. The Amazon Straightforward email service is professional as well as IT experts to access as well as send email.

Other providers

Amazon Web Services includes a assortment of productivity for businesses

SaaS options. Its Amazon Chime service empowers text-based conversations across different devices as well as calls and video-based meetings. Companies can make use the benefits of Amazon WorkMail, document sharing and storage support and Amazon WorkDocs that have calendaring features.

The streaming services for programs and desktop are part of Amazon WorkSpaces as remote platform. Also, Amazon AppStream is a service that lets programs to be streamed from AWS to stream from a programmer to the end-user's browser.

The most frequently utilized AWS solutions

1. Amazon EC2

Do not worry about the costly physical servers by using the Amazon Service, which lets us create virtual machines that handle the various characteristics of servers, like ports, security, storage and more.. With Amazon EC2, andyou can build servers with an operating system.

You'll be able to work and you will have to manage your servers.

2. Amazon RDS

Amazon assists in the creation of an infrastructure system that is complex. This is that it provides all RDS support our way. But what exactly can it offer? With this support and service, we'll have completed database cases in less than a minute completely handled by AWS support group. AWS support group. They are as well as able to support several databases, such as SQL, PostgreSQL, SQL Server and more...

We will not forget all the days of caring and service on our databases!

3. Amazon S3

What happens when I use the cloud to my personal information? Amazon S3 provides Once we discuss information, the infrastructure they use provides steady and secure. Alongside intelligently distributing data across multiple areas and integrating features like PCI-DSSand HIPAA

FedRAMP and / and HITECH and HITECH, which ensures that our data won't ever be at risk.

That's?

Absolutely not, AWS S3 offers high accessibility. The data you need is just one click away, and with almost zero latency of 99.9999999999 percent. Perhaps you're wondering how this event is going to be? We're happy to inform you that it's. First of all, it's an absolutely free product that includes 5 GB of storage . It prices start at $ 0.023 per month, up to the initial 50TB.

4. Amazon CloudFront

Maybe you've wondered how fast your site loads? When users join your site do they have to wait minutes to launch the website? Along with the global Content Delivery Service, Amazon is responsible for making it available, handling your content, and also introducing it economically. With the integration of AWS along with latency and other services.

5. Amazon VPC

Is my data in danger within AWS Cloud? AWS Cloud? The answer is no. Your information will only be to be available to programs or to the individuals you have authorized. Alongside AWS VPC, you may create a private digital network in which your entire information technology environment (services as well as infrastructure) is kept away from the outside world. This way your data isn't exposed to any kind of exposure.

6. Amazon SNS

To address the programming problem, AWS provides us a special notification system that allows integration with every program that is PHP, Python, Node and so on.. Any platform, we can notify our customers via Amazon SNS, whether it's mobile or web-based.

7. Amazon Elastic Beanstalk

This is the service that caters to programmer. As an engineer, you wouldn't want to manage your website's infrastructure, don't you? It's normal because its maintenance is difficult and boring to tackle any problem. This allows you to focus on creating software or the applications they create, and programmers must manage the infrastructure.

8. Amazon Lambda

Are your waiters flooded with demands? You don't know What to do? Don't worry about the evolution.

If you like the majority of programmers are faced with the problem that your infrastructure isn't able to support the demands of your work, AWS Lambda is the solution for you. This allows you to work in a setting that offers support. You manage the programming. Everything is working and AWS is accountable to provide the necessary tools and climbing at the same at the same time.

9. Amazon Auto Scaling

AWS's magic - pick it to extend our service to millions and the tens of thousands of users?

And, once again, we're being answered by Amazon. With AutoScaling, we can manage a number of servers capable of supporting the amount of traffic that our program requires. The ceremony is completely free. the only thing that has changed is the amount of cases.

10. Amazon Elasticache

Memory.Elasticache is compatible with Memcache as well as Redis.

"Now you've got the skills is required do not be deceived. and set out to create amazing things using AWS along with ClickIT."

AWS pricing model and contests

AWS provides a cloud version of its cloud Solutions that can be accessed on a per-second or per-hour basis. You can also purchase a set amount of computing capacity with a fee for customers who purchase only one or pay in full or take on usage responsibility.

If the customers are unable to pay for the cost, AWS Free Tier is an alternative method of utilizing AWS services. AWS Free Tier allows users to gain the experience for free with AWS services. The users begin to build on AWS and can use up to 60 items. Free Tier is available through three ways: trials for 12 weeks free, and of course, always free.

AWS competes with IBM, Google, and Microsoft Azure From the public sector that is infrastructure-as-a-service.

What is AWS Cloud Computing

AWS is the most hated term used in IT Technology. Amazon Internet Services is known as AWS and is considered to be remote service that provides cloud-based infrastructure through the internet's packages. It's provided using specific storage bandwidth, bandwidth, and a custom service that works with the Application Programming Interface (API). It was introduced in the year 2006 and has become the world of cloud-based service providers. The AWS cloud mostly uses the subscription pricing model that's or pay-as-you-go pay-for-what-you-use.

What is AWS Cloud Computing?

Amazon Web Services is manufactured by combining a variety of Cloud offerings and. Here's the Amazon branch which provides servers, networking storage, remote computing mobile, email, protection and development. It could be split into two primary products comprising S3 as well as the Amazon Virtual Machine Service, Amazon's storage platform and EC2. It is divided into 12 regions, where various availability zones are placed on each server. The functioned zone is classified so that constraints can be set by users to the services.

"Most of these Organizations are buying on AWS Cloud to Boost Organizational Revenues"

Alternatives and all of the cloud services are to build applications that are flexible as well as scalability, reliability, and. It's an Broad IT Infrastructure system which offers a range of infrastructure-related services, including databases, storage options and networking possibilities in the event of a need for utility.

AWS Cloud - A Broad IT Infrastructure Platform

The Platform to Use Cases

*Deep Characteristics and How to Benefit out of the Day

* Security functions that are stronger than those on premises

* A deep look into Governance and Compliance

How to Start with AWS Cloud?

Measure 1. AWS Subscribe

If you want to have access to, you have to sign up to AWS Amazon's cloud computing solutions, with the requirement for a credit card in order to complete the process.

Step 2: Launch the Application

You can make use of AWS for hosting and the CloudFormation template allows for the capability of launching WordPress websites.

Step 3: Ask For Assistance

Acquire assistance that is fantastic from AWS Technical Service Engineers through AWS Support. You can also find the AWS Solution Provider from an ecosystem of independent Software vendors and System Integrators.

What is AWS EC2?

Amazon EC2 (Elastic Compute Cloud) among Amazon Internet Services' providers provides companies with the ability to run applications in the cloud. Programmers can design examples of virtual machines , and take advantage of the potential scaling cases by using the interface provided by EC2.

EC2 allows users to create apps.The following features make it simple to set up servers and manage storage , changing demands and peak times, reducing the demand, while aiding in streamlining development processes.

EC2 installation requires the creation of the Amazon Machine Picture (AMI) The programs include an operating system as well as settings. The AMI is loaded into S3 of the Amazon Simple Storage Service (S3) and is registered with EC2 after which users can create virtual machines as they require.

Amazon offers case kinds of EC2 Budgets and requirements like hourly, booked and price-per-spot.

Amazon Characteristics for EC2

Attributes and Advantages are based on computer scientists' programming. They include:

Response to the changing requirements for capacity Simple Growth issues that occur when programs demand to scale up. Scaling of EC2 reduces the amount of money.

Flexible settings for The size of memory can be set by the user, boot dimension of the partition and CPU optimization they choose.

Integration EC2 as well as AWS providers are able to integrate, for example, RDS, SimpleDB, and SQS.

Management: Users have access to instances, and can block and then allow access to output while also conserving boot partition information.

Security: Users can decide which cases are secret and which ones are open to disclosure. EC2 requires Amazon Virtual Private Cloud (VPC) to protect users and businesses can link their safe IT infrastructure to sources of VPC.

Price Pricing: One of the pricing options, EC2 offers hourly low rates.

Controlling EC2 Clusters Using ECS

It is the EC2 Container Service (ECS) makes use of EC2 cases to provide an Effortless and fast method. This reduces frustrations and makes it containers as the basis of an application.

It is therefore likely to be similar to EC2. Its ECS support is simple to scale up to adapt to the increasing capacity demands of the application. It permits monitoring of the batch procedure for services and software. It also provides integration with applications as well as AWS products.

Information about Amazon The EC2 (Elastic Compute Cloud)

Amazon Elastic Compute Cloud (Amazon EC2) is an online service that allows companies to run applications from Amazon Web Services (AWS). Amazon Web Services (AWS) cloud. Amazon EC2 permits a programmer to build virtual machines (VMs) that the capacity to calculate cloud-based workloads and IT jobs that are able to work alongside the world's AWS Data centers.

Chapter 4: The Benefits From Amazon Web Services

Amazon Web Services gives an array of features that make it different from similar to other firms. They include:

1. Access to Portable Friendly

It is a combination of two ways: AWS Mobile SDK and AWS Mobile Hub.

AWS Mobile SDK

AWS Mobile SDK underpins Android, React Native, IOS, Unity, Web, etc. With the help provided by this feature, it's possible to connect to many Amazon Web Services, for instance, Lambda, DynamoDB and AWS S3 (Simple Storage Service).

AWS Mobile Hub

The Mobile Hub helps the application to become an appropriate and effective element for the application. It is possible to design screens, test, and build your application using the reassure that is included in the.

Other features like message pop-up messages and content transport are also provided through AWS's Mobile Hub. AWS Mobile Hub.

2. Easy to Use

As opposed to different levels, AWS gives an easy stage to use in which the apprentice is able to benefit from it. It's possible to do this because of the clear documentation and the helpful support AWS provides.

The most well-known course in this class

Digital Week Sale

Distributed Computing Training (18 Courses and four+ projects)

18 Online Courses, 4 projects that are hands-on 100+ hours Lifetime Access

4.5 (2,360 reviews) Course Price

$39 $599

View Course

Related Courses

AWS Training (9 Courses, 3+ Projects)Azure Training (5 Courses, 4+ Projects)

3. Secure

Amazon Web Services gives a basic and secure platform where clients pay only for the services they utilize. It offers a broad range of security-related services. Character Access and Management (IAM) is one of the services that allows administrators to control access for clients to use AWS administrations. In recent times, Amazon Web Services presented tools that assess security risks naturally. Additionally, it offers devices with encryption (both software and equipment), Transport Layer Security endorsements, security from Distributed Denial of Service (DDoS) attacks and channels of destructive traffic to applications. The Amazon Inspector device Amazon Inspector can be used to examine a user's Amazon Web Service cloud organization and then to detect vulnerabilities and security threats. In addition Amazon's private cloud allows users to make instances private or public based on the needs of their customers.

4. Capacity

AWS offers high stockpiling that can be used free or as a combination of. The stockpiling capacity is high. EC2 instances can support clients in the event they're using any of the high-input/output application like Hadoop, Data warehousing, and so on.

Amazon provides a variety of stockpiles, such as:

Amazon Elastic Block Store (EBS) Stockpiling at the block level which can be used in conjunction with Elastic Compute Cloud (EC2) cases, which assists in keeping track of the data.

Amazon Glacier: Used primarily for stockpiling long hauls in which information that's not used regularly is stored away. In the sense of capacity for the reinforcement of information and for chronicling.

Amazon Simple Storage Service (S3) helps in providing the ability to stockpile via an electronic interface.

Amazon Elastic File System storage is used to help with the burdens and the applications available for those who are caught in the general fog that are part of Amazon Web Services.

Capacity Transport Equipment: For reasons of business, Amazon gives certain capacity equipment, like Snowmobile and Snowball that can be transported beginning at one location and moving on to the next. Snowmobile can move lots of data using trucks that carry a variety of hard drives to keep petabytes of data. Snowball is a tool for moving data throughout AWS and costs one-fifth less than the cost of moving across the internet.

5. Pay Per Use

In contrast to the other stage, Amazon web administrations don't require the user to pay for each and every one of the services accessible within the platform. It charges only for the resources, stockpiling and capacity to transfer data they use. In light of this it's the largest part of business segments from AWS when compared with other types of.

6. Multi-Region Backups

Amazon provides a handful of districts in which customers can store their data and files. These districts have accessibility zones that are safe from being a victim of disappointment in other areas. The main reason for Multi-Region Backups is to dispatch the EC2 instances in any region to guarantee that clients' applications work. If the zones are situated in the same region, it is possible to organize the dormancy process and keep costs lower. Locales could be located in separate geographic territories, provinces and other provinces and. Customers can select the region that is indicated by their hotel. In addition, a Cloud Ranger (outsider assistance) thus reinforces the information throughout the various areas.

7. Incredibly high-quality and scalable

Amazon offers a framework which is scalable based on the usage. As a result, the cost of use is reduced in the event that the customer reduces the models that they use. As of today, it is mentioned under the term "pay per usage". It is the ideal solution for large enterprises since they do not have to deal with additional assets in the event they're running short of capacity.

Chapter 5: Web Developer Services

If you're writing software You'll need to be aware of the web developer's services and the reasons why they're important. We'll go over the web development tools, and the services you'll need, and the benefits you'll get from them.

API Gateway

API gateway allows you to redirect APIs of an application via the service, which handles traffic, as well as testing new versions of the. In general, you can label it an API Proxy. API Proxy

What it means to developers is straightforward by allowing developers to develop, maintain the APIs, track, publish, and secure APIs themselves. It is possible to develop WEbSocket or REST APIs which act like an "front door" to run applications that allow you to access your business logic, data and functionality. It also handles back end services, too. It takes care of all the duties involved in processing the millions of requests that are made through the API and how the traffic is managed, authorized and the control's access and, from there, you'll have the ability to control and monitor the entire process. Additionally, it doesn't require the minimum costs or start-up expenses, and you only have to pay for calls made and transfered out, so you'll save on the costs of this.

In essence, the way this functions is that users connected as well as applications IT devices and private apps like VPC have a command to go into. Amazon API gateways receive theseand, after that, the users connect through the Data Center private applications , or any other AWS to interact using them.

RDS

RDS is a term used to describe regional database services. it assembles an application that allows you to expand the regional database in your cloud. It offers a cost-effective and expandable capacity for the regular regional database and takes care of the typical tasks. In essence, it functions as a regional database , taking care of the backups, patches to software, automatic failure detection and recovery. Additionally, you could use it in conjunction together with other replica software for this.

Route53

Route53 is basically a means to buy the domain of your choice, and lets you set up your DNS Records for your site.

What it can do for ordinary users is that it offers developers a cost-effective method of connecting users to apps by changing name into IP address to allow them to connect to other users. It is also able to connect to other requests from users for running AWS also.

SES

SES allows you to send one-off letters, like changing passwords, providing notices and other users. Many use it as newspapers, but it's best to send details to your customers.

This applies to digital marketers, application developers, as well as the such to their customers. Sending out email campaigns can be quite irritating however, when you have the SMTP interface installed on this you can incorporate it with other programs to allow clients to send emails to other customers.

Cloudfront

Additionally, you have Cloudfront which is great to speed up the loading time of websites. It speeds up the loading time of websites and allows static files to be shared with users. For numerous clients, it's important to observe how fast or slow the loading times of a website are. Slow websites make it difficult for customers to view it. However, Cloudfront lets the site to be displayed immediately after users click on it.

Cloudsearch

This program lets you access all of the data on the S3 or RDS and then search for the information you need. It allows you to establish a system to search, and to have options that are available. It's not necessary to fret about how you've already put it there previously. In essence, all of the capabilities that the system will be made available in order for users to benefit from it. The search parameter, the relevance and even new settings are available at any point and it is possible to adapt to the demands of your.

DynamoDB

This function lets you scale the keystore of the application.

What this means is that it's an application that can provide performance that is scalable to any size. What this means can be seen in the example of Lyft, AirBnb, and Redfin They'll be able to increase the performance to match the most efficient workloads as well as ensuring that customers are guaranteed the highest quality service they can get. This application is able to manage all queries and queries, which is great for those who don't want to manage the triad of requests on your own.

Elasticache

Elasticache is fully managed Redis and Memcached. What this means is that it uses to run, scale, and manage the most popular open-source compatible storage systems. This allows you to develop applications that use data to enhance the performance of applications that are currently available by retrieving information from the high-quality data storage facilities that do not have delays. If you're running game applications This is an excellent option to stop the service's latency.

Elastic Transcode

The elastic transcoder lets you format different issues in different videos, and similar videos. Perhaps, for instance, you would like to convert all the video footage in the format of a thumbnail. From there, it will aid in doing this and make it much easier. It is usually difficult to achieve without the help of an AWS flexible transcoder, and it allows you to put this all together in a very simple way and without the hassle of code. This is always a plus for those who want to run these kinds of applications. It lets you convert all types of media files. Furthermore, it is capable of the transcoding process, managing and fine-tuning the system, and also supports the most popular outputs.

SQS

SQS is a basic queue service. This means that it is able to queue up information so that it can process it in a sequential manner. For instance, if you have lots of requests for services, and you're unable to manage them using the current software in exchange for paying the information is saved in a queued form which means you don't need to manage this and making it simpler for you to.

WAF

WAF is essentially an firewall that is employed to block all unsafe website requests that are secured by Cloudfront. It is also useful for protecting passwords and doesn't permit anyone to access any of the passwords with sensitive information that are stored here.

You can also select whether or not you want to disable the application. then you could also design patterns that permit you to respond quickly . This will enable you to develop deployment, and ensure the security rules in this manner, and as always, you pay only for the services you actually use.

Web development is a must, and each the AWS services let you make the most of this, and aids in making even the most complicated of websites. So you can create useful applications that other users could benefit from.

Chapter 6: Of The Amazon Appstream Security Guideline. Amazon Appstream Security

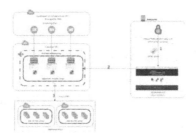

It is the Amazon AppStream service provides frameworks. to run the streaming app which is a specific application, it requires a tiny application to working on mobile devices. you can save and run applications on GPUs that can perform large-scale parallel processing, and provide great efficiency in cloud, and then stream them to your device.

Output and input data can be sent to any device, no matter already-existing apps that you alter to use Amazon AppStream or an application specifically made for the service.

Amazon AppStream SDK Amazon AppStream SDK simplifies the development of interactive streaming applications as well as client applications. The SDK comes with an API.

It will connect to the device of the user straight to the program. recording and encoding audio and images. The streaming content that is available online is as real-time decoding of content on mobile devices. The client can also transmit input from the user to the application. Because the application runs in the cloud, it support scalability in order to manage processing load. The capacity can be massive. Amazon AppStream uses the streaming application that runs on Amazon EC2 when you add streaming applications via Amazon's Management Console.

The service will generate an AMI that will be required for hosting the app as well as allow the application to work by streaming clients. It will also be extended.

Applications are available as required within the limit of capacity you define. Adjusted to meet the requirements of users who use apps that use the Amazon AppStream SDK will automatically connect to the streaming app generally, however, it is important to ensure that the user running the client is authorized to use the app prior to giving an ID for the session. We suggest using the service for certain types of authorization, which verify the identity of the user and allows access to your application. In this scenario the authorization service can also be used to call an Amazon AppStream REST API to create the new streaming session on behalf of the user. When the service is completed, the authorization to make a new session the session's identifier is given to the user that is granted a URL that has the one-time authorization. The client is then able to use the URL that has authorisation to join the application. Authorization is stored in Amazon EC2 Instance or on AWS Elastic.

Beanstalk

Amazon AppStream uses the AWS CloudFormation template to make it necessary for the application to utilize an GPU EC2 instance with the AppStream library.

Windows Application and Windows Client SDK is installed and configured automatically with access via SSH, RDC or VPN and to provide the flexibility of assigning IP addresses for this template. To utilize a streaming server that is standalone. All you need to upload the app to the server and execute Command to turn it on. The Amazon AppStream Service Simulator tools to test the application in a the standalone mode before deciding whether they as the actual work system. Amazon AppStream also uses the STX protocol to handle applications streaming via AWS on specific devices via the STX protocol.

Amazon AppStream is an private protocol that makes use of high-quality video streaming for applications. It is a network that has various characteristics, it also checks its characteristics, it can adjust the stream of video in real time to minimize delay and higher resolution for customers as well as synchronizing audio and videos and keeping input data of customers to be sent back to applications running on AWS will be faster and less time-consuming.

Service to analyze

Amazon Web Services provides cloud-based analysis services that assist you in processing and analyzing the volume of data. Whatever you need to manage Hadoop real-time streaming is the best option. petabyte data warehousesing, or any other operational processes

Amazon Elastic MapReduce Security (Amazon EMR)

Amazon Elastic MapReduce (Amazon EMR) is an managed web service is able to be used to call an Hadoop cluster to process data. There is a lot of work and data is dispersed across multiple servers using the most advanced variant of Apache Hadoop framework running on the same structure that is used for the web-scaling capabilities of Amazon EC2 and Amazon S3 You simply upload your input data and applications for data processing to Amazon S3 Then, Amazon EMR will start activating its Amazon EC2 Instance for the amount you choose. The service will begin running the process while extracting information.

Input via Amazon S3 into active Amazon EC2 instance. After the workflow is completed, Amazon EMR will transfer the output information into Amazon S3, which you can access or use the information to create other workflows. When the workflow is activated for you. Amazon

EMR will set up the Amazon EC2 security groups in two distinct groups. The primary one and the second group. The primary node is equipped with an open port for communicating to the service. There is also an accessible SSH port that allows you to utilize SSH to connect to the instance is running using the key you that is set at the time of system start-up. primary node is an additional security group which can be used only with the primary instance in accordance with the default setting the settings of both security groups. an option to not allow access from other sources, such as the Amazon EC2 Instance belonging to customers.

Additionally, these security groups are part of the account. modify the configuration the account using EC2 tools or traditional dashboards. Amazon EMR protects customers' input and output data sets using SSL in order to move data from and to Amazon S3.

Amazon EMR lets you manage access to resources in the cluster in a variety of ways. You can make use of AWS IAM to set up user roles and accounts and set permissions to control the capabilities of AWS are accessible to users and the roles they play. If you enable the cluster, you can connect to the Amazon EC2 key pair to the cluster. This is utilized when connecting to the cluster via SSH. You can also assign permissions to allow other users.

Users who are not using Hadoop can submit tasks to cluster on a regular basis. However If any the cluster IAM users is enabled the other IAM users within the AWS account will not be able to access the cluster. This filter works through the interface all the features of Amazon EMR including CLI, consoles APIs, SDKs and consoles and can help stop IAM customers from accessing clustering changes and clustering them on behalf of users.

Another IAM was created accidentally that is compatible with the cluster to be viewed by one IAM user and the primary AWS account. There is also the option to make it mandatory for all IAM users with one AWS account to view and access the cluster.

To add an extra layer of security, you can activate EC2 instance of the EMR cluster inside Amazon VPC. Amazon VPC, which is similar to activating subnets.

Therefore, you have complete control over subnet access. You can also activate the cluster feature within VPC and grant the access to internal resources network by using an VPN connection. You can also encrypt input data prior to uploading into Amazon S3 using the encryption tool.

General information in case you encode your data prior to uploading it, you must include the decoding procedure at the beginning of the workflow process when Amazon Elastic MapReduce retrieves data from Amazon S3.

Amazon Kinesis Security

Amazon Kinesis is a managed service that manages streams of information from Amazon several of them in real-time that could receive lots of information . You can use Kinesis in a variety of ways and can be expanded and modified according to the need.

Data processing in many real-time situations, such as log files for social media servers, or marketing feeds, and also information on clicking on links on web pages. The application can read and write data records into Amazon Kinesis in streaming. You can make multiple streams of Kinesis to save.

It can store and transfer data. Amazon Kinesis manages the infrastructure Storage Network system as well as the configuration necessary to gather and process data automatically in the form of streaming applications. required. You do not need to think about the preparation, deployment or maintaining.

Continuous versions of software, hardware or any other service to be capable of saving information and store it in a database. of which are in real-time Amazon Kinesis can also model data at three different locations in the AWS region simultaneously for high availability and long-term data retention.

Within Amazon Kinesis, data records include sequences of keys, partitions and data blocks. They are bytes which do not change and do not require to be understood. This is because the Amazon Kinesis service will not analyze or modify information contained in blogs. No matter what the characteristics, data records are available at any time, but only 24 hours.

The time has passed since you added it to the Amazon Kinesis stream, and will be automatically deleted. Your application is a member of the Amazon Kinesis stream, which typically works within the Amazon EC2 Instance group. The Kinesis application makes use of an Amazon Kinesis Client Library to read the Amazon Kinesis Kinesis Client Library stream, and will take all the information for you.

In addition, it allows for switching between to load balancing and recovery that allows the application to focus on processing when it is it is ready to be used after processing the records the user's ID can be sent using another Kinesis stream, and written to Amazon S3 buckets.

Redshift and DynamoDB table can be deleted. You can utilize Connector library in order to connect Kinesis together with the various AWS products (Such like DynamoDB, Redshift, and Amazon S3), as in addition to other products from third parties such as Apache Storm.

You can manage the logical access to Kinesis resources and management functions through the creation of users using AWS accounts that make use of AWS IAM. You can also regulate what actions are performed by Kinesis users who are able to assist in the development of applications for both users and manufacturers in Amazon EC2 Instance. You can set up the instance using an IAM function, and it provides the AWS credentials that demonstrate the rights associated with that role.

IAM is a good option to use by applications in a variety of situations, that means you don't need to utilize long-term AWS Security ID.

Roles also have advantages due to the fact that temporary identification expires after a short period of time , which provides greater security options. Check out the details on the IAM role in IAM's IAM guide for users.

Amazon Kinesis API can be accessed via the data is encrypted with SSL (kinesis.us-east-1.amazonaws.com) to help ensure that secure data is sent to AWS. You need to be connected to that data in order to connect to Kinesis however, you are able to utilize the API to direct AWS Kinesis.

Chapter 7: What Is Cloud Computing?

Basically, distributed computing is the conveyance of processing administrations--including servers, stockpiling, databases, organizing, programming, investigation, and insight--over the Internet ("The Cloud") to offer quicker development, adaptable assets, and economies of scale. The typical cost is for the cloud services you utilize to reduce your operating costs, and running your foundation more efficiently and expand when your business's requirements change.

Top Benefits of Distributed Computing

Distributed computing is a significant shift from how companies think about IT assets. Here are seven typical reasons that organizations are deciding to distribute computing administrations:

Cost

Distributed computing removes the expense of buying equipment and programming, and then making it ready to go in nearby datacenters, the racks of servers and the continuous power supply for cooling and power, and IT experts to deal with the base. It includes quick.

Speed

The majority of distributed computing services offer self-help upon request, meaning that massive amounts of figuring assets can be set up in a matter of minutes, typically in just a few mouse clicks. This gives organizations an abundance of flexibility and taking the pressure off quantifying the scope.

Global Scale

The benefits from distributed computing services are the ability to scale up and down. In the context of cloud computing, this involves transferring the best amount of IT assets, for instance, quite lots of processing power, storage speeds for transfer--right when it is needed and from the most appropriate geographical area.

Profitability

On-location datacenters typically need lots of "Racking and stacking"-- arranging equipment as well as programming repair, among other interminable IT tasks. Distributed computing eliminates the need for a lot of these activities, which means IT departments can focus their efforts in achieving increasingly crucial business goals.

Execution

The most effective distributed computing services operate on an overall network of data centers that are secure, and typically are upgraded to the most modern version of fast and efficient registering equipment. This has several advantages over a single corporate datacenter. These include less application idleness and greater scale efficiency.

Unbeatable Quality

Distributed computing makes reinforcement of information as well as disaster recovery and business growth easier and less expensive because of data is reflected in a variety of different locations within the cloud provider's system.

Security

Cloud providers offer an extensive array of techniques, innovations and security controls that increase your security, generally, protecting your applications, information and even your foundation from threats.

Kinds of Distributed Computing

There are many mists that are not the same and no one type that uses distributed computing will be applicable to all. There are a variety of distinct types, models and administrations have been developed to offer the right solution to your specific needs.

First, you must choose the type that of cloud or distributed computing model that cloud services will be based on. There are three different ways to transmit cloud-based administrations in open cloud, a private cloud, or half and half cloud.

Open Cloud

Open mists are owned and operated by an outside cloud specialist organization that transfer their processing resources like servers and capacity through the Internet. Microsoft Azure is a case of an open cloud. In an open cloud, everything you need to know about programming, equipment and other infrastructures are managed and controlled by the cloud provider. Access these administrative services and manage your account using an internet browser.

Cloud Private Cloud

Private cloud refers to the use of distributed computing resources by a single company or an association. Private clouds can be physically located on companies' datacenters in the location. Certain companies can also hire outsider specialists to host their own cloud. A private cloud is where the administration and the framework are managed in a secure system.

Half and Half and Cloud

The half and the half-mists are private and open mists connected by technology that permits information and apps to be shared among them. By allowing information and applications to transfer between open and private mists, the half breed cloud offers your company more flexibility with more options for arrangement and strengthens your existing base security, consistency, and security.

Chapter 8: Benefits Of Aws

Often, people ask for convincing arguments as to the reasons they should consider AWS as their foundation requirements. Despite the fact that hundreds of thousands of customers who have an impact on AWS more than 180 countries, there are a variety of context-based analyses, including companies like Netflix, Pinterest, Dow Jones, SAP, Coursera NASA/JPL, Reddit, Vodafone, 99Designs, Thomson Reuters, Flipboard, Expedia and LinkedIn yet most people who manage their foundation on their own or through an established server farm with a co-founder might be facing concerns regarding security, cost, protection , and a few other.

On this post, I've written down what I consider to be the top 10 benefits of using AWS to meet your foundation requirements:

1. Zero CapEx:

A lot of people will generally agree that AWS or any other cloud-based system is only reserved for the wealthy. However however, the reality is opposite. We consider AWS as a leveler of the playing field that allows new businesses to utilize top quality technologies and essential foundation requirements and foundation needs with ZERO CapEx. Businesses that are new and do not want to use Oracle for their databases or any other plugs or virtual products that require a high-forthright authorizing fee should look into AWS Marketplace. In high-likelihood they will discover these products in an hourly model that does not require any cost.

2. No-Commitment:

No matter if you need an internet server to host the creation of a tiny website or you need a Content Delivery Network (CDN) to provide large traffic destinations an incredibly flexible and adaptable email management or information warehouse management or a Hadoop group to meet your BigData requirements, AWS offers everything with absolutely no commitment of the imagination, and not in any way for a month. Server-supported services are charged by the hour that means when you shut down or stop the server, you will not be charged for the hour later.

3. The Disposition of Negotiations:

Value exchanges certainly aren't a place of expertise for all (at at least for me) and no one of us enjoys spending our time and energy in this endeavor regardless of the necessary skills. AWS is primarily focused on making it easier to lower the costs of foundations for their customers. They've reduced their evaluations across different services over multiple times in the past few years. Tools like Trusted Advisor, or outsider tools like CloudCheckr, Cloudability, Cloudyn and more can offer some insight to increase the cost of your current arrangement with AWS.

4. Acquisition:

In order to acquire a new server, you'll need an investment of between some hours to eight or ten days, based on the nature of your foundation: on-premise co-founded or if you have an affiliation to a facilitator. The same time frame is required to obtain programming licenses too. However, AWS empowers you to launch new servers in just a few minutes without any reason for you to buy separate licenses for certain frameworks that work and programming projects.

5. Payment Per Us:

Consider unbounded space for your reinforcement and authentic needs, the capacity to dispatch new servers, up-scale/downscale a server, CDN combination, transcoding media records, boundless data transfer capacity and a lot more profoundly adaptable administrations/highlights accessible to you while you pay depends on your real use as it were.

6. Security:

AWS has developed a world class extremely secure framework both on the physical and internet. AWS has a few features to choose from. security measures mentioned on AWS website are:

Server farms are monitored 24 hours a day with security monitors that are prepared and access is granted in a careful manner on a least specific basis

Different geographical locations and Availability Zones allow you to be flexible with the most frustrating of scenarios such as catastrophic events or frame failures

Ability to organize worked-in firewall rules from completely transparent to completely private or somewhere in between of limiting access to certain events.

Influence Identity and Access Management (IAM) and CloudTrail to ensure that the track is connected to all exercise sessions conducted by different clients.

The few other features are private subnets, multi-factor verification (MFA) Isolate GovCloud and scrambled info storage.

7. Adaptability:

Do not ignore the mystery or use logical analysis to identify your foundation needs. Auto-scaling can be used to build a self-overseeing foundation which is adjusted in line with the real requirement based on the usage of assets and traffic. Amazon Machine Images (AMIs) lets you create replicas in different districts for different conditions in a matter of minutes, eliminating the need to repeat the setup steps repeatedly.

8. Worldwide Leader:

Amazon has global connectivity with its 10 districts with 36 accessibility zones, and more than 50 edge zones. In the last few months Gartner placed AWS in the Leaders Quadrant of the new Magic Quadrant for Cloud Infrastructure as a Service. Gartner further stated that AWS is more than more than the limit used, which is higher in comparison to the totality of the 14 other companies that are set in the same Magic Quadrant.

9. Top tier PaaS Offerings:

AWS has come up with amazingly adaptable and flexible administrations of oversaw for database and reserving, information warehouse transcoding, capacity strengthening, foundation of the board, and application executives, which decrease the amount of time and effort that is required to set-up and deal with the framework. In this way, significantly decreasing the process of going from demo to showcase for the end-users.

10. Interface for programming:

APIs are available in a variety of programming languages to aid in the management of your framework on autopilot. Whatever the case, whether it's pushing another application forward or gaining reinforcements, the sky's the limit with API. It's true that APIs have more power over those using the AWS Management Console.

Six Benefits of Cloud Computing

Capital cost of exchange for variable cost. Instead of investing heavily in servers and server farms before you are aware of what you'll do with these resources, you pay for only the amount you use up registration assets and only pay for the cost you use.

Benefit from massive economies of scale. By making use of the distributed computing model, you are able to achieve a lower variable cost than if you were to jump in a single. Since the use of a vast amount of customers is gathered through the cloud, the providers like AWS are able to achieve greater economies of scale. This results in lower follow-through on the as-you-go cost.

Stop speculating limits - Get rid of any speculation regarding your framework's limits. When you decide on the limit option prior to sending your application to the world, you often find yourself sitting on inactive assets that cost a lot of money or managing limits that are constrained. When you use shared computing, all these problems are eliminated. You can use the system to as an extent or a amount as you require and expand in the right places in a matter of seconds' notice.

Rapidity and agility In an environment of distributed computing new IT assets are one click away, which means that you reduce the chance to make these resources available to your designers , from weeks to just minutes. The result is an increase in emotional agility for the company because the cost and time required to develop and test is significantly less.

Stop wasting time running cash and managing server farms . Focus on projects that are separate from your company from the framework. Distributed computing allows you to focus on your clientsinstead of the work of racking or stacking servers.

Get your message out to the world in a matter of minutes. Simply share your message across the globe in a variety of locations all in few clicks. This allows you to offer less inertness and an excellent experience for your customers for a minimal cost.

7 Benefits of AWS AWS For Cloud Computing Demands

Due to the growing trend of organizations moving their I.T. framework to cloud computing there are more possibilities for distributed computing administration than ever before in the past.

This trend doesn't appear to be slowing down anytime within the next few years. Moving to the cloud can offer an investment opportunity that is quick and frees you from the burden of having and running servers.

According to a study conducted by IDG Enterprise, cloud innovation is now a norm for businesses as 70% of the largest companies having in every case one application on the cloud. (2016 Cloud Computing Survey)

As we've mentioned before There are a myriad of alternatives available, but according to our perception nobody can compete with Amazon Web Services, the leader in the cloud management for general use area, Amazon Web Services

(AWS). Amazon is the biggest of companies on the planet as clients: Adobe, Comcast, PBS and Dow Jones (just to give an example.)

This is a list of seven benefits that your company can benefit from by using AWS to manage your cloud-based applications.

7 Benefits of AWS AWS

1. Exhaustive

Moving from stockpiling on location to the cloud is an essential step for AWS because of the progress they've developed in training and preparing. Cloud powerhouse has an array of information on their website, including documents and exercises to help you starting using AWS as well as their numerous administrations, and that's just the top of the Iceberg.

AWS additionally offers an Partner Network, which is made up of professional companies that assist clients to create, design, build and manage their most challenging tasks and the applications available using AWS.

To be granted our status as a counseling accomplice Lofty Labs representatives passed a couple of accreditations and affirmations, have client references on AWS and had proof of earnings through AWS administrations.

2. Practical

It doesn't matter if you're a small or large undertaking company, you'll save money by utilizing the services your company requires at a unintentional time. AWS has concentrated on estimating it's just a fraction of what on-premises plans cost.

You can assess the costs of running your apps on-premises or colocation conditions to AWS with this nifty device for computing.

3. Flexible

No matter if you're moving to the cloud simply because you want to, or shifting from a different cloud management, AWS has every one of the resources you need to improve your I.T. framework. The framework supports the idea of the ability to scale assets either up or down and down, meaning your company does not have to worry when there is you're facing a problem or when requirements shift.

4. Security

Checking for potential security breaches and hacks is an essential requirement for AWS. They offer well-known consistency evidence and stick to their commitment to protecting lAWS all over the world.

Nasdaq, Dow Jones, and HealthCare.Gov all utilize AWS as an indication of how secure AWS can be as a secure cloud management system.

5. Better Productivity

AWS is a great way to AWS to boost your distributed computing means removing the risks and obligations that come with to lodging at an I.T. foundation. It also reduces the need for I.T. boost staff, and will save your business time and money over the long term.

6. Creative

There are numerous articles which state that it's Amazon's dedication to innovation, not that the aggressive evaluation process that finally prevails on their customers. As they fight a valuing war between Microsoft as well as Google, Amazon still can't be seen to overcome rivalry in its commitment to innovation and the development of. According to a participant at the recent AWS reinvent Conference in 2016, AWS launched nearly 1000 new administrations just a year prior to that.

7. Worldwide Leader

Amazon Web Services works in around 190 countries and has more than a million active customers. They look over some of the largest and smallest companies around the world as clients and can even assist those in the open sector.

Benefits of using AWS Cloud for Business

What exactly is AWS Cloud and how might it benefit your company?

One aspect of the advantages companies should be thinking about using in the AWS cloud.

AWS is also known as Amazon Web Services, is an Amazon said distributed storage arrangement that offers a wide range of benefits for entrepreneurs. AWS is described in the words of Amazon by stating that it is "Offering an extensive array of global registers and stockpiling system, database examination, application and sending services that help businesses in speeding up the process of moving their applications and with lower IT costs, and to scale applications." Here's a brief overview of the services offered via AWS and the benefits for business from AWS. AWS cloud.

Versatility

AWS provides advantages that are affordable for businesses, all things all things being the same, from brand new enterprises to companies with significant traffic. One benefit of moving into the AWS cloud is that it allows you to evolve with your business. It also can aid in growth by providing the flexibility of a cloud-based platform and web-based business capacity solutions that boost your company's.

Duty-Free

One advantage of using Amazon cloud-based services is that, regardless of the AWS management your company is there is no commitment or agreement to secure with them and there's no minimum expenditures required to make use of their services. The server-based services are all constantly charged, meaning that once you have ended the service or use of servers, you're never ever charged again. This is applicable to all organizations of size and can be beneficial for anyone who is concerned about paying too much for capacity they don't want or having to sign an agreement with a service or management that doesn't meet their needs.

Security

AWS administrations are more efficient and robust security features that include:

Every minute of the day access to specialists should issues are likely to arise.

Was part of the firewall that takes into account the obvious access to information, ranging from impossible to access

IAM administrations that monitor clients ' progress to

Multiple verification options and scrambled data capabilities for stockpiling

As information stockpiling and security are such a crucial aspect of businessissues, when switching to a cloud provider or an administration stockpiling service is a good sign that security will be the most sought in the first place and AWS security is robust enough to protect most businesses.

Dependability

Amazon has a vast reach and an enormous collection of tech experts that have helped them build a solid server structure that has proved to be stable and reliable. Many organizations have secure and reliable relationships with information which help them build create their business bases. This exceptional capability makes AWS an appropriate choice for certain organizations.

Flexible and customizable

AWS allows you to select your programming language the working framework databases, as well as other sources, so that you are able to make the best arrangement for your organization. There's no guarantee in the case of a new program which ends in costing your company time and money rather than opening up resources that will help you grow and strengthen your company. This kind of flexibility paired with Amazon's renowned simplicity and simple to use stage appeals to certain companies.

Why is AWS betterthan other storage options? It provides a speedy and flexible, secure and a budget-friendly solution for many companies looking for a distributed storage solution or application that has. Many sellers benefit from using the AWS cloud, and made use of this easy-to-use stage to aid their business IT requirements. Have you noticed any benefits from AWS cloud-based services? If not Have you even thought about AWS or other cloud-based arrangements?

Prologue to the Benefits of AWS

Amazon Web Services (AWS) is a cloud-based platform with benefits that are safe and provides administration like content transfer control calculation, stockpiling databases and more. It assists in selecting the database dialects, programming dialects as well as working frameworks, applications stages, and various options based on the needs of the client. Nowadays, a variety of businesses, such as Nokia, Airbnb, Netflix, Slack, and Samsung are using this platform to fulfill various business requirements because of its small number of areas of significance. Let's look at the benefits from AWS in the following section.

Benefits of AWS

Amazon Web Services gives an variety of benefits that make it not identical to other firms. These include:

1. Portable Access for the Blind

It combines two different ways AWS Mobile SDK and AWS Mobile Hub.

AWS Mobile SDK

AWS Mobile SDK underpins Android, React Native, IOS, Unity, Web, etc. With the aid from this part, it's possible to access various Amazon Web Services, for instance, Lambda, DynamoDB and AWS S3 (Simple Storage Service).

AWS Mobile Hub

The Mobile Hub helps your application to be an appropriate and effective part for your app. It is possible to develop screens, test, and even test your application using the reassure feature, which is available within it. Other features like message pop-up messages and substance transmission are additionally provided through AWS Mobile Hub. AWS Mobile Hub.

2. Easy to Use

As opposed to different levels, AWS gives an easy stage to use in which apprentices can also benefit from it. It's possible to do this because of the distinctive documentation and helpful support AWS offers.

A well-known Course in this class

Digital Week Sale

Distributed Computing Training (18 Courses and 4+ projects)

18 Online Courses 4 hands-on projects 100+ Hours Achievable Certificate of Completion Lifetime Access

4.5 (2,360 scores) Course Price

$39 $599

View Course

Related Courses

AWS Training (9 Courses, 3+ Projects)Azure Training (5 Courses, 4+ Projects)

3. Secure

Amazon Web Services gives a basic and secure platform where the customer pays just for the services they make use of. It offers a broad range of security services. Character Access and Management (IAM) is one such service which allows the administrator to manage access to customers for the use of AWS administrations. In recent times, Amazon Web Services presented tools that assess security risks naturally. Additionally, the company offers tools that include encryption (both software and equipment), Transport Layer Security endorsements, and protection against Distributed Denial of Service (DDoS) attacks as well as channels for destructive traffic that targets applications. A device called Amazon Inspector can be used to examine a user's Amazon Web Service cloud organization in order to identify security risks and weaknesses. Additionally Amazon's private cloud enables clients to keep instances private or public based on their requirements.

4. Capacity

AWS provides high stockpiling that is available free or in combination with. The stockpiling capacity is high. EC2 instances can support the user in the event that they're using any of the high input/output software such as Hadoop, Data warehousing, and so on.

Amazon provides a variety of stockpiles, such as:

Amazon Elastic Block Store (EBS) Stockpiling at the block level which can be used in conjunction with Elastic Compute Cloud (EC2) cases, which assists in keeping track of the data.

Amazon Glacier: Used primarily to stockpile long-distance stocks where information that's not used regularly is stored away. In the sense of capacity for the reinforcement of information and for chronicling.

Chapter 9: Amazon Web Service Security

Numerous polls have revealed how security concerns are the top most important concern about cloud computing as stated in the opinion of IT professionals. Many IT users are skeptical of cloud service providers' security and think they have the sole authority who are capable of implementing safe computing systems. There are many kinds of IT are the most skeptical about AWS security. Many of them have not even mentioned it however, a significant part of their resentment towards AWS is I believe, a sort of disdain for AWS, based on the belief that"booksellers "bookseller" isn't capable of providing the same type of computational protection as "real" professionals offer.

Clouds can also have boundaries. The primary factor in understanding cloud security is understanding the notion that confidence limits. The IT department is responsible for the security of the entire cloud in the on-site computing environment which you may be familiar with, regardless the level or which part a specific security requirements are in place. In contrast, in a public cloud environment. Only a small portion of the security scenario is implemented and accepted by the provider.

Here's a great approach to frame the debate The concept of a trust boundary establishes a clear distinction between the responsibility that the company's service providers have and your obligations. The service provider handles securities on the one hand of the boundary and on the other side that is the boundary of trust you are accountable for the security.

This definition isn't exclusive to AWS in any way. If, for instance, your business uses Salesforce to manage the customer's interactions Salesforce has the responsibility of the entire system for substantial security. In actual fact, when you use the services of an external service and you are responsible for that service, you owe it an obligation to protect. The primary problem in these instances is how to distribute the burden with the service provider.

So , the most crucial question regarding cloud computing is where the trust boundary reside? In a sense, when using the case of a Software as a Service (SaaS) service such as Salesforce the trust boundary has to be placed in a location where the bulk of the security responsibility lies with the service provider. After everything, Salesforce not only runs the computing environment that the application operates and develops, but also creates the application, distributes it, and takes responsibility for the application.

The trust boundary being placed in the instance indicates that Amazon is responsible to ensure the safety of the computer environment components:

1. The physical structure is the data center, access control for the people who work there and all electrical power as well as cooling and internet connectivity and network connections starting from the outer perimeter of the building all the way to the computer equipment

2. Computer hardware: All computing, storage and networking devices.

3. The hypervisor, the instance manager, as well as the virtual machines that run instances are run.

4. The core software infrastructure software is what manages the entire AWS resources. It also provides capabilities to work with the application without the need to talk to another person

5. The application programming instruction The application programming order stated the security of your data is shared obligation and there are certain aspects of security that rest in your hands.

6. Software packages to support your application include all the software used

to create your application, as well as the components of the software that you create.

7.Configuration of your program to ensure the security of the program, setting up software programs properly is essential to make sure that no shady person can gain access to them and cause destruction.

The operating system that runs an application (possibly) is: This is a bit complicatedand is directly connected to my previous description of the security obligation "starting at the level of an hypervisor" as "a little glib." It's all dependent on who's accountable for the image you utilize. If you're using an image that was created by an individual (either Amazon or a third partner) the security of the operating system as well as the bundles that comprise the operating system are at the disposal of the image vendor and includes not only the operating system in general (e.g. Windows 2008 or Ubuntu Linux) as well as all patches for an operating system the system software (e.g. the identity management software) and possibly the middle of.

This is the Deperimeterization of Security

In assessing the different requirements for security, then you might have to take into consideration the consequences of a concept referred to as security deperimeterisation.

(Of course, you'll need to consider what is the proper way to approach an expression you're unable to say?) Let me provide you with some background information: the concept of deperimeterisation originates from the work of Jericho Forum. Jericho Forum, an industry research institute that is a an integral part of The Open Organization. The fundamental belief of the Jericho Forum's founders is that traditional computer security methods, which concentrate on protecting against threats that are located at the edges that surround the data centre are inadequate in today's computer environments.

The rise of frequent attacks from state and criminal actors with the use of covert installations and monitoring ongoing by Advanced persistent threats (APT) and the ever-changing malware and viruses that create the risk of zero-day threats (dangers which require immediate action instead of waiting until updates are made to the virus scanner database or other malware-detection tools) You should never be confident that security measures that are implemented on the outside of your computer resources are adequate.

Jericho Forum Jericho Forum recommends that everyone be aware of the success of security deperimeterisation and, consequently, acknowledge that:

1.Security measures must be implemented on every device used for computing.

2.These interventions should be able to protect the property, without relying on security solutions that rely on external boundaries. Amazon does not require you to install an IDS/IPS system on their network due to

135

3.It will find this behaviour unacceptable for its operation as well as for the regulations it needs for proper operation of AWS.

4.Additionally is that others AWS customers might consider your device to be an attack on their security applications. Any surveillance system that monitors traffic is considered an intrusive tool by any other user who attempts to examine their own traffic and would consider it unacceptable.

Installing the host-based intrusion detection system such as HIDS, for AWS instances AWS cases is the best way to solve the issue. (The IDS letters also include IPS. Even techie types would be uncomfortable with an acronym like HIDS or HIPS.) HIDS is essentially the same function as an IDS / an IPS appliance, but it does not permit any device to be installed on the network.

How will deperimeterisation affect the vital line of trust that separates your own area of responsibility and that of Amazon? It's not is the case, to be honest.

Deperimeterisation is the context of what's happening , but it doesn't change the basic character of the relationship you have with Amazon because

1. Amazon is still the sole authority for all computer-related security, right up to even the hypervisor. In reality, as I mentioned earlier, this statement is not completely accurate since Amazon is the one responsible for the creation of the virtual machine and its operation. In addition, Amazon is also responsible for the security of the image in the event that you're making use of AWS files. AWS file.

It's up to you to make sure that the proper operating system update, as well as all necessary updates and appropriate modifications are made. Amazon manages and manages all software and hardware It doesn't need to worry about AWS security (and in fact, you can't do anything).

2.You remain accountable to ensure the safety and general use of the running case.

This applies to all software used within the case, regardless of whether it was designed through you (or your company) as well as a third party vendor (commercial or open-source communities).

You can customize and control the entire program You can customize the entire program, and Amazon does not have anything to do with it. (Indeed that it shouldn't be doing anything since accessing your data could be a serious breach of trust, and an acceptable reason to make customers abandon the program.) But, in one area both you as well as Amazon have a shared responsibility in security, and that's at the point where Amazon's domain of responsibility and yours. In a way, this refers to the interface between networksthat is where traffic from the network departs from Amazon's network and flows into yours.

Aws Security Groups

Each instance comes with the AWS virtual network interface and Amazon creates a software firewall for each instance. The firewall helps with the management of traffic to and from the instance.

Each instance is able to launch an firewall that is locked to the wall by default, meaning it is blocked from traffic entering the area. As you can imagine, this can render it ineffective when it is not performing computer activities that are self-contained.

Therefore, you must be able to allow access to your instance via the network.

(If you've had the misfortune of using the Linux security device, don't worry: Amazon makes the job easier by utilizing security groups.)

The following aspects of access to network traffic are controlled by the safety community rules:

1. Network protocol: Security group agree and refer to three kinds of network traffic protocols:

* Transmission Control Protocol (TCP)

*Users Datagram Program (UDP): This network protocol that is simpler is more straightforward than TCP is rarely used and therefore you are able to skip it.

*Internet Control Message Protocol (ICMP) This protocol is utilized to support certain command for monitoring networks and also to transmit error messages for applications.

2. Source of traffic: Its purpose is to track the sources through which security groups receive traffic. (My assumption is that you don't make use of this protocol often also.) The security group may be configured to allow access from all IP addresses, only one IP address, from a variety of addresses or even from other members of the security group.

3. The traffic port, TCP moves between ports, which are viewed as individual network connections in the network's overall connectivity.

Most ports are linked to specific applications, and all traffic that goes through one particular port is directed to the application. Port 80, as an example is used for example to support internet traffic (or specifically, HTTP traffic).

One would like to limit the flow of traffic on a port to one application. in the event that two applications attempt to read traffic from the network on the same port, there are issueswhich port is the data to be sent?

Security Groups

Each account is associated with a single security group defined that is default. This defaults with no traffic being allowed into the instance, therefore it is impossible for any traffic to reach the instance at every time you begin an instance that has the default security group that determines which network traffic is allowed.

You can also create more security groups and add rules in the security groups you create. AWS accounts can have up to 100 laws. AWS account can hold up 500 security groups per security group, and 100 laws.

Security group rules to allow traffic to an instance, you need to open some or all ports by setting the default security rule for the group. For example, you could make a rule that allows the entry of HTTP traffic to the instance.

The law is clearly able to be enforced using The AWS API. The majority of people make use of AWS Management Console to determine guidelines. AWS Management Console to determine the guidelines.

Security Group Best Practices

Since it performs a crucial role The security group serves a vital function. crucial feature. It controls the flow of traffic through your applications. Knowing and implementing security groups is crucial for ensuring the correct and secure running of your software. Use this list of the most effective security group practices:

1.Remove the Security group Default. Even though the default Security Group may open ports, it is best to do not use it. make separate security groups for any traffic rules that are applicable to networks instead. It's a waste of time to make use of default settings, and leads to poorly designed structures and practices.

2.Use famous names. If you choose names that offer useful information it is much simpler to determine which security group to use in which situation. It might not seem too complicated, but I assure youthat you'll appreciate any help you get when you are managing more than 100 security groups.

3. Simply open the ports you require access to. Cloud computing does not have anything to do with this well-known suggestion. The reduction of the number of ports that are open minimizes the risk of being targeted by malicious agents, so you should you should only open ports for features or applications that you need.

4. Applications that require partitioning. Utilizing security groups to divide applications is a sensible procedure for implementing scope protection , and it could be a way for malicious actors to gain access to critical applications' resources.

You should ensure that you create security groups that support the different versions of the application will be running. Limit access to the administrator system. You can restrict administrator access to the instances using CIDR masks, and to the computers that are located in places that you are confident about, like your office at work. If employees work from their homes or are on the road to work, you can create an Virtual Private Network (VPN) that connects their devices to your corporate network. You can then forward the traffic to the AWS system administrator through on the network of your company, which it is in line with the CIDR masking you've implemented.

Chapter 10: Getting Started With Aws

With the above details, it's time to begin to explore AWS. There are the fundamental starting steps here to guide you towards the proper direction. Keep in mind that AWS offers a variety of free tutorials accessible on their website and if you decide you want to learn more about the subject or think you require something that isn't listed in this guide.

Create an EC2 instance

One of the most fundamental features within AWS includes that of the EC2 service. It is necessary to establish this service in the beginning. Once you've logged in to your account, you'll be in a position to go ahead:

Click on to open the AWS Services tab in the upper left corner of your screen. You will see choices to select one of AWS Services in their respective categories including Compute, Storage and Content

Delivery Networking Developer Tools and Management Tools as well as Security & Identity. Click on Compute.

Then, you'll need to click EC2 in the Compute category. After that, you'll be directed into the EC2 dashboard. The dashboard contains everything you require to set up an instance, in addition to any information regarding instances that are currently operating or using EC2 currently.

Take a look at the top-right part of the EC2 dashboard. Click on the region where you want your EC2 server to be provisioned. The region you select will be 10 to select among: US East (N. Virginia), US West (N. California), US West (Oregon), EU (Ireland), EU (Frankfurt), Asia Pacific (Tokyo), Asia Pacific (Seoul), Asia Pacific (Singapore), Asia Pacific (Sydney), and South America (Sao Paulo).

* Once you have the region selected, go back on your EC2 Dashboard. Then, look for the blue button that reads Launch Instance within the Create Instance

header. This will trigger the wizard for creating an instance to open for you.

Select AMI

In the next step, you're required to select one of the AMI (Amazon Machine Image -- the template for an operating system). This will allow you to choose the foundation for your instance to run every time.

1. The standard AMI will be Amazon Linux 64 bit. This is the default AMI for now , if you're following this tutorial.

Select the EC2 instance types you prefer.

You must now select which type of instance is best suited to your company's needs. There is a huge table that lists types, family, VCPUs memory (GiB) Storage for instances (GB) EBS-Optimized compatibility, as well as Network Performance. Check these out to determine which one is best suited to your needs.

*Click on the checkbox next to the instance type and then click Configure

Instance Details at the lower rightmost box.

Configuring the Instance

* You are allowed to provide an maximum of 20 instances at any one moment. In this guide, we'll keep a single instance, but it is recommended to use whatever is suitable for your requirements.

After that, you can check out the Purchase option just below the box in which you typed in your number of times. At this point you can leave this box unchecked.

In this stage, you'll be setting up information. The first step is to select the VPC you would like to use to start the instance on, and then select the subnets you want to use. Be aware that this needs to be planned before you begin creating the instance to ensure ease of arrangement.

Under the option to purchase there should be an option to select the network, then the subnet and then the auto assignment of public IP. Focus on Network for now.

You can choose one VPC which you have already established, or you'll require a new VPC. Choose the one that works best for you. After you have selected your VPC You will be required to select or create a subnet. After this you will be assigned an IP that is public in this case.

* If you don't desire the IP to be generated automatically for instance, the case if you wanted to do it manually then click the dropbox to select the Auto-assigning Public IP and select "use subnet setting, enable,' or disable.'

You now have the option of assigning to an IAM role or even create one. In the meantime, you can you can leave it as is.

* Shutdown behavior will follow. You must decide if you would like the shutdown behaviour of your instance to end or to end (delete). Most people do not want to delete everything and will instead choose the option to stop. To protect yourself you can choose to enable termination protection by selecting the box.

When you look at Monitoring, you have to decide whether you would like to pay for additional CloudWatch monitoring, or if you are not interested in to pay for it. Keep in mind that basic monitoring is available for free. However, in the event that this is something you are concerned about you might want to sign up.

* The next step is the issue of. This refers to whether you share your hardware or run an application independently or launch it from a dedicated server to secure it. If your application is secure or requires high security, choose dedicated Tenancy.

* This is the final stage in the process of configuring. Nowis the appropriate to create storage.

You can add Storage for your EC2 Instance

* You will notice that the SSD was assigned automatically to general-purpose SSD (gp2). Then, you can alter it to the one you think will meet your requirements most. You'll be able to select between Provisioned-IOPS and General Purpose SSD or Magnetic (HDD).

Tag Your Instance

In this stage, you can label your instance, if needed. This is a case-sensitive pair which allows an AWS admin to become seen despite the number of instances. If you're going to tag multiple people here, it is recommended to try giving them a title that reflects their role and their environment to ensure maximum convenience and accessibility. For instance, you could tag them with "Dev" to indicate that the tag is intended specifically for developers.

* Once you have created the tags (you can create as many as 10 tags) then go to the lower right corner and select next: Configure Security Group.

Configuring Security Groups

In this section, you'll be able configure security. You can decide to limit traffic by, for instance, permitting an additional firewall to be set aside that of an OS firewall that was installed. You may choose to make use of the older group of security, or create an entirely new one.

If you want to start a new website first, you need to create an initial name along with an explanation.

Then, you must define the protocols you are willing to allow, along with the IP addresses can access the server. If you are running a private server, you could set it to restrict access to an IP address; however when it's something that is public, it would be best to make it be accessible from all places.

The access to the administrative area is identified by SSH instead of HTTP, HTTPS or both. This should be restricted to your IP as well as the IPs of all other machines that need this access.

If you are happy with your configuration then go to the right-hand corner of the screen and click the blue Review and Launch button.

Review Situations

Review your selection to make sure they're in your preferred style and then hit"Start" in the blue button at the lower right corner.

Then, you need to create an encryption key pair to allow you to access your account. AWS requires to download your private key. Do this and keep it secure and backup it in case you lose it, you'll never have access to it in the future. The process is as simple as creating an encrypted key pair, assign the key a name and then download the key and save it to an encrypted folder.

Launch Instance

Then Click to the Launch button in blue.

* This will show your Launch Status which allows you to view what it is currently doing.

The launch log will be displayed in a green box so you can see what took place.

Click on Instances in the left-hand panel. It will show an instance's status and you'll be able to notice it beginning with "Pending." This will then change into "running," and you can see the private IP offered by AWS.

Create an EIP, and connect it to your instance

It is the EIP refers to the fixed IP that AWS offers, and means elastic IP. Your instance will be assigned an IP address that is public when it is started, however this will change constantly. If you want to create an IP static that could be used to connect to your instance via other networks, you'll require an EIP.

* On the left side in the EC2 Dashboard, you need to scroll towards Network & Security and select Elastic IPs.

Then, click the red Allocate New Address button at the top of the screen to the left side, just below the dashboard.

* Assign the IP that will be utilized in VPC rather than EC2. As long as you have less than five EIPs in your account it will pass through and create an elastic IP for your account.

You must now give the address to your instance. Begin with selecting that EIP that was created, and then checking the box to the left. Next, you must go to the gray Actions box, and then select Associate Address.

* It will take you to a different page on which you have to look for the specific instance you want to link and then select. You must then click the blue Associate button.

In this moment, you should be on your screen of instances and you'll be able to see it using your EIP.

* Open PuTTY in your list of programs , and then enter the EIP in the Host Name (or the IP Address) box.

* Next, you need to insert the private key that you downloaded to secure your connection. The left-hand dropbox look for SSH and then expand it then move to the AUTH. The private key has to be uploaded to the server in .ppk format. This means you have change the format of your file AWS to .ppk by using PuTTYgen.

* Click Open. It will open a Linux prompt. Remember that this won't function if the

machine you're using is configured to be part of part of the security group SSH.

* EC2 must now be enabled as server.

AWS Comprehension Practice Test

In this section, you will be tested on your understanding of the content that has been presented to you so far. Consider this an opportunity to assess your comprehension of the text. These questions will come in different formats, and you'll be able to view the answers in the next section.

1. True or false The cloud is accessible when the weather conditions are favorable.

2. Which is the safest form of cloud: private, public or hybrid? Why?

3. What is the basis of the different types of cloud computing that are at the base of the stack of services?

a. Serverless

b. Software as a Service

C. The infrastructure of a Service

D. Platforms as Service

It is. hardware as Service

4. What exactly is AWS utilized to do?

A. Hosting applications

b. Social media

c. Media distribution

D. A & C only

E. A and c.

5. Amazon EC2 signifies:

a. Essential cloud compute

B. Cloud computing cloud with elastic compute

C. Control of the cloud's elevation

d. Essential control catalog

6. False or true: Amazon EC2 runs on instances.

7. What exactly is Amazon S3 for primarily?

a. Selling I/O credits that are not used

b. Storage services

C. System configuration

d. System configuration

8. Which system of storage in S3 is designed to be used for storage over the long term?

A. Amazon Reduced Redundancy Storage

B. Amazon Infrequent Access Storage

C. Amazon Standard Storage

d. Amazon Glacier

9. ELB means:

a. Expanding latency barrier

B. Barrier to load that is elastic

C. A. Elastic load balancer

d. Expanding latency balancer

10. ELB is vital as it:

a. It safeguards the function of an application when the EC2 instance is not able to function.

b. It makes the load on the application networks to the level they are able to handle.

C. It's made to prevent high levels of latency that can be escaped from contro.l

D. Each of the mentioned

E. One of none mentioned

11. CloudFront offers one of the following services:

a. The monitoring of information from a variety of applications

b. Offers graphs of real-time data

c. Tracks source IP information

D. Each of the mentioned

E. none of these mentioned

12. False or not: HDD is faster than SSD in processing and accessing information

13. True or false: Provisioned SSD IOPS (io1) can be described as the most efficient of EBS options.

14. False or true: CloudWatch Detailed Monitoring is absolutely free

15. What are the purposes in AWS Lambda?

a. Creating code for you

b. managing servers

C. Debugging and correcting the program

d. Streaming videos

E. none of these mentioned

16. How do you decide on the kind of EFS storage you'd like to use?

a. By speed

b. By volume

C. By the frequency of access

D. By the type of memory you wish to access

17. What kind you would like to use for Amazon Kinesis would you want to stream video?

A. Amazon Kinesis Data Streams

B. Amazon Kinesis Video Streams

C. A. Firehose

D. Amazon Kinesis Data Analytics

18. What exactly is what is a VPC?

a. Very Private Cloud

b. Virtual Public Cloud

C. Very Public Cloud

D. Virtual Private Cloud

19. What are the most significant advantages of DynamoDB?

a. Serverless

b. Global

C. Secure

D. Scaled

E. Each of these previously mentioned

F. The above are not the case.

20. True or false: The primary step in creating the personal AWS is setting up an flexible IP address.

AWS Comprehension Practice Test Answer Key

This list provides answers to the questions previously asked. To determine your percent right, you should give yourself one point for each correct answer, and then multiply your score by five.

1. False: Cloud refers to being digital, and not connected to the sky.

2. Private--It's only accessible by people who have access to and are granted access to the specific cloud.

3. C

4. E

5. A

6. True

7. B

8. D

9. B

10. D

11. E

12. False - HDD is faster.

13. True

14. False: The Basic Monitoring is for free.

15. B

16. C

17. B

18. D

19. E

20. False: First, you need to create an instance.

Frequently Answered Questions

What are the benefits of using AWS?

There are a variety of reasons to consider to select AWS: it is simple to use, and offers complete control, and lots of customization. This makes it extremely adaptable, and economical. It's also flexible, reliable and extremely secure, due to the an international infrastructure. Numerous big-name firms are using AWS because of its reliability, cost-effectiveness and user-friendliness.

Why is everything flexible?

Elastic storage and applications allow users, you the user to pay only for the amount you actually need without having to calculate how much, guess or estimate the amount of storage you require. When you're in need of more, it's there to you. As you make use of less, for instance, deletion of certain items, it will shrink down. This will prevent you from paying for functions or storage which aren't being utilized or from being unable to store data.

Why should I choose serverless computing?

If you choose to use serverless computing, you'll avoid the need to spend time making sure you are configuring your server to work with the program you've written. This allows you to instead concentrate on running your program and making tweaks to your code instead of providing with tech support.

How can I tell if I should go with HDD-backed or SSD-backed storage?

It is mostly based on speed. SSDs can offer faster speeds, and consequently lower latency than HDDs however they come at a price. SSDs cost more to make and operate than HDDs and, therefore, should you opt to utilize an SSD storage device you'll experience faster speed, but it is at a greater price. You should conduct your own cost-benefit analysis to determine if it is worthwhile to pay the extra expense.

Do I have my data secured? What happens in the event of an emergency?

Yes--your data is quite protected. Except for Amazon Reduced Redundancy Storage, generally, there is some degree of redundancy which allows your data to be stored across multiple location, providing the protection of a catastrophic event.

What are my options for protecting my personal information?

Data is secure by infrastructure, which includes physical safeguards to protect data as well as operational measures to protect and monitor the data, and software safeguards that protect the data. Check out CloudWatch for instance to learn about the ways your data is protected from damage.

How do I calculate my price?

This is heavily influenced by the product, volume of processes, as well as other applications and is mostly distinct. It is possible to view current pricing rates on the AWS website under the pricing tab.

Do you provide discounts?

There are occasions when you can qualify for discounts based on volume. That means the more you use the less you will have to pay per GB. S3 is one of the best. It is priced according to GB use.

Do you have a Customer support program?

You are legally entitled to some basic support simply by being a member of access to an AWS account. If you select one or the premium support programs, you receive an additional support services. For instance the developer plan permits for general guidance or system-impaired support during office hours in the hour or so. The enterprise plan provides 24/7 support and responses of 15 minutes when critical systems for business have failed or aren't functioning properly.

Chapter 11: Aws Versus The Rest

AWS is a market leader in the cloud hosting competition and is a top contender thanks to its unique solutions, services and flexible payment arrangements and worldwide coverage.

This chapter looks at how AWS stands out from the other cloud hosting options available currently available.

Microsoft Azure

Microsoft and Amazon cloud services could be a tough choice as both are popular cloud-based solutions.

In terms of configuring EC2 against Azure's preconfigured VMS from Azure, AWS EC2 gives the greatest flexibility as it can be set up in real-time. Azure's VMS requires users to select a virtual disk. This VMS is then configured by a third party. That means the user is required to provide the particular memory or cores required to run the Azure VMS environment.

AWS provides an adaptable and flexible temporary storage option This storage is only allocated only when the instance being initiated requires it. If the instance no longer requires the storage, it's destroyed. In the case of Azure clients, Microsoft offers temporary storage however, it is referred to as block storage. Storage for objects in Azure the storage is performed by using Blobs. For block storage, this is done through Blobs while for VMS storage, it's accomplished through page Blobs.

AWS Virtual Private Cloud operates through allowing the user to build separate networks in AWS's AWS cloud. Azure is an virtual network that can create isolated subnets and allocates Private IP Address ranges and also networks. This is basically similar to AWS VPC.

Azure is more flexible in the case of the hybrid cloud system. Azure generally stays away from cloud providers that are third-party.

In their pricing model, AWS and Azure both utilize a pay-as-you go pricing system. However, AWS costs per hour whereas Azure is more likely to charge per minute, which makes it a more strict pricing model.

AWS includes a host of other features as well as services and configuration options that are flexible. It is easy to customize and offer many options through various tools made available by third party. However, Azure is quite easy to use by almost everyone who can make use of Windows. Customers can build the cloud hybrid to be used in create an in-house Windows server.

The two AWS and Azure both have plenty of services to provide their users but the decision on which will depend on which one best fits the requirements of the business. AWS offers Infrastructure as a Service (IaaS) as well as a broad range of services and products. However, if you're seeking Platform as a Service (Paas), Azure has a many advantages.

Rackspace

Rackspace and AWS have been in existence for the same time and Rackspace is an extremely popular cloud hosting platform. AWS EC2 and Rackspace offer the same services, using pretty all the same tools. The only difference is the pricing structures, and Rackspace is reported to be a little higher priced than AWS.

In terms of infrastructure services, AWS EC2 and Rackspace are quite like. Both platforms offer a wide range of low-cost solutions and services. AWS provides more the developers with regards to tools and resources, with the Cloud9 IDE and ECS container platform service.

There are managed services provided by Rackspace that are not provided by AWS. You can, in fact, get managed services from Rackspace for support AWS infrastructure.

As a multi-cloud system can be easily utilized Rackspace managed services, while taking advantages of making use of

AWS EC2 instances. Since these companies are introducing new capabilities, running multi-cloud environments are getting more and more popular. This is because you can enjoy the top of cloud-based hosting.

With a bit of management capability and the tools needed it's not too difficult to implement multi-cloud systems.

Google Cloud

The decision of AWS or Google Cloud is a tough one, since each have their strengths and drawbacks.

For larger businesses with established requirements, AWS would be the most suitable of the two options. AWS is a global company which makes it an ideal choice for multinational businesses who require an option that extends over Europe and the United States and Europe. AWS is also equipped with the latest security options, is greater resilience, and can provide an excellent quality of support.

However, Google Cloud has sweetened the pot by offering a large free tier offer. It also offers more range of flexibility than AWS and comes with one of the lowest rates for cloud hosting services. Google Cloud also has an a wide range of options for customers to choose from.

If you wish to benefit from the capabilities offered by Google Cloud and/or Azure along with AWS the two, it is possible to do this accomplished in a multi-cloud setting. A multi-cloud setup allows users to select each cloud hosts that meet your requirements.

DigitalOcean

There isn't much competition when you compare DigitalOcean against AWS. This is due to the fact that DigitalOcean has a distinct customer base. DigitalOcean is geared towards smaller developers that require instances or instances that aren't too big however able to support high-performance systems.

AWS is a much bigger company that provides cloud hosting service on a wider size, with a focus on the bigger market with mixed and hybrid environments.

DigitalOcean is a good choice to beat AWS when it comes to VM performance, offering users a user-friendly interface that's basically a blank new slate to begin working on. Additionally, they offer limited services that don't overload their customers with the massive array of services AWS provides. They also offer developers the ease of deployments with one click.

When you combine AWS IaaS or PaaS it is possible to have a myriad of amazing services to select from. It's as exciting as it is difficult for the user. If you're not a developer seeking a simple and fast service, AWS has more to provide. However, as a group they're not businesses that can be compared as they each provide the customers different solutions to meet their specific requirements.

IBM Cloud

IBM is in IT business for a longer time than Amazon. They've gone from huge mainframes and AS400s to the latest technology. It is only logical that when they come to business solutions, they'll provide AWS an opportunity to compete for money by offering cloud hosting.

IBM also is the name of their brand which gives them an competitive advantage, since their name have become associated with computers. IBM does have advantages over AWS in cloud hosting due to its flexibility in settings, its monitoring systems and management tools.

Yet, AWS has the advantage due to the huge variety of solutions and services it offers at very affordable prices.

Oracle Cloud

In terms of cost, Oracle cloud has the advantage over AWS due to their pricing-to-performance being available for certain services. Apart from that both are alike in the sense that Oracle cloud is ideal for the requirements of large corporations. The two IBM and AWS provide high-level safety, security, and scalability as well as hybrid applications. For Oracle applications it is possible that the Oracle cloud might be the ideal solution because both Oracle and AWS provide a wide range of appropriate solutions for developers.

VMware

It is impossible to be comparing VMware Cloud and AWS or AWS, at least not because they've came together to form an alliance in which AWS was hosting VMware Cloud. VMWare Cloud. This is a completely fresh dimension the two companies, AWS as well as VMware. AWS users now get access to an on-demand service that provides vSphere Cloud-based services. VMware is capable of offering its customers more than just applications in the vSphere cloud, but additionally access to the broad array of AWS services.

The service is run via the VMware Cloud Foundation. It provides all the well-known VMware tools, including VMware VSAN, WMware vCenter management, VMware vSphere, as well as VMware NSX. IT teams that are experienced with VMware will have no trouble controlling this VMware cloud-based systems. The IT team's standard VMware software has been adapted to work on the AWS an elastic cloud infrastructure. This infrastructure is provided in a private cloud providing the customer with all the advantages of an entirely dedicated AWS pure-metal cloud.

Together, AWS as well as VMware have developed a powerful tool that makes use of both cloud environments, both public and private which can benefit both businesses.

CloudWays

CloudWays is a cloud-hosted firm that is popular with people looking for a speedy reliable, simple, and affordable solution for cloud hosting sites. As opposed to having to wade through the technical jargon when setting up cloud-based hosting, CloudWays gives a simple easy-to-use solution. It can help someone who has limited technical skills use a framework that is technical like the pros.

Customers also have the option to host their websites with all major cloud-based hosting firms which includes AWS. CloudWays acts as the intermediary between users who need cloud computing, but aren't highly technical.

Alibaba Cloud

A few users outside China have heard of Alibaba Cloud that was the main cloud-based market until. However, Alibaba Cloud is fast becoming a major player to reckon with in the cloud hosting industry. Alibaba Cloud has been around from 2009 onwards, just two years later than AWS.

Alibaba Cloud mainly focused on China and its neighbors until a massive cash injection into the company enabled it to expand its reach to its first target, the United States. The company was officially launched within the US in the year 2015 and shortly after it extended its reach across Europe during the year 2016.

Alibaba offers the same features similar to AWS as well. Their pricing structure differ based on the service or service required.

Although Alibaba is able to provide most of the services for its customers as AWS can but it isn't so well-known as an established brand. Alibaba isn't currently able to boast the geographic reach as AWS has, but Alibaba is planning to expand its geographic coverage in the near future. Alibaba could soon be closely with the giant of the world, AWS.

Conclusion

Amazon provides a variety of online services. A lot of them are mentioned in this book.

In simple sense, refers to processing and storing data as well as services via the Internet and not on the hard drive on your personal computer.

Your hard disk is the thing cloud computing doesn't concern. This is known as local computing and storage when you save data to or run applications from your hard drive. Anything you require is located close to your and you'll have quick and easy access to your information (for this particular device or on networks that are local to you). Utilizing your hard disk is the way that the technology industry has operated for the last decade.

Computing technology's future is on the cloud. This means that if you're not adjusting your business to the cloud-based model, your company is going to be behind in this age of advanced technology.

Cloud computing occurs when companies collaborate on a network of accessible servers. Servers are hosted on the Internet and allow organizations to manage their information "in the cloud" instead of the local server. It's a virtual area that devices connected to the network are able to access data from any place.

Cloud computing has just gained momentum in the past two years in the last decade or two, the idea was in use for a long time. John McCarthy, a renowned computer scientist, first introduced the concept when he developed a method that would allow computing to be sold as a commodity , similar to water or electricity. He stated that subscribers will only be charged for the amount they actually utilized and that specific users could offer services to others.

Amazon Web Services (AWS) Introduction to Famous Amazon Web Services is an extremely robust cloud platform created by Amazon's online retailer. It provides software-as-a-Service (SaaS) Platform-as-a-Service (PaaS) as well as infrastructure-as-as-a-Service (IaaS) solutions. Take a look at the history of electricity to comprehend the logic behind AWS.

In the beginning, factories will construct their own facilities to power their factories. In the course of time, both private and public investors have built large power stations that provide electricity to many cities, factories, and homes. With this new system factories will be charged much less per unit due because of the scale economies facilitated by these massive power plants. AWS was developed and constructed using similar principles.

In the year 2006, Amazon had established itself as the world's biggest internet retailer. A position it holds to this day. The seamless operation of such an operation demanded a massive and complex infrastructure. Amazon was equipped

Amazon with deep knowledge in managing large-scale networks and servers.

In the end, AWS was created in 2006 when Amazon endeavored to make available to individuals and companies the technology infrastructure it built and the experience it gained. AWS was among the first pay-as-you go (PAYG) computer models to increase the performance as well as storage and computing according to the changing demands of the users.

Amazon Web Services offers cloud infrastructure that includes many data centers as well as various accessibility zones (AZs) covering regions across the globe. Each AZ comprises a range different data centers. Customers can create virtual machines and replicate their data across several AZs, resulting in high-performance, scalable networks that is invulnerable to server or problems with data centers.

AWS offers a variety of cloud services that are centralized to create applications like analytics block chain, AI, etc. This can help both companies and individuals in the creation and growth of any kind of application. These are the primary components in AWS. AWS system.

AWS EC2 Elastic Compute Cloud, also known as EC2 is an online server that allows you to run a variety of applications using AWS's AWS cloud-based infrastructure. It lets users run applications within a computer environment that is capable of hosting an unlimited variety of virtual machine.

With AWS the only thing you will get are instances with various processor resource settings, memory storage and networking. Every model is offered in various sizes to meet the demands according to the requirements. The instances are via Amazon Machine Images (AMI). These computer images serve as a model that defines the operating system and define the user's operating system. Users can also set up the AMI themselves.

www.ingramcontent.com/pod-product-compliance
Lightning Source LLC
LaVergne TN
LVHW051233050326
832903LV00028B/2383